INTRODUCTION

This Snapshot guide, excerpted from my guidebook *Rick Steves' Ireland,* introduces you to Northern Ireland—an underrated and often overlooked part of the Emerald Isle that surprises visitors with its friendliness. I've included a lively mix of cities (Belfast and Derry), smaller towns (Portrush and Bangor), and plenty of lazy countryside sights. History is palpable atop the brooding walls of Derry and in the remote and traditional County Donegal (actually just over the border, in the Republic of Ireland). And, while it's perfectly safe for a visit, Northern Ireland gives you a feel for Ireland's 20th-century "Troubles" as nowhere else—especially the provocative political murals in Derry's Bogside neighborhood, and on Belfast's Falls Road and Shankill Road. But you'll also find enjoyable escapes: From the breezy seaside resort of Portrush, you can visit the scenic Antrim Coast—which boasts the unique staggered-columns geology of the Giant's Causeway, the spectacularly set Dunluce Castle, and a chance to sample whiskey at Old Bushmills Distillery.

To help you have the best trip possible, I've included the following topics in this book:

• **Planning Your Time,** with advice on how to make the most of your limited time

• **Orientation,** including tourist information (abbreviated as TI), tips on public transportation, local tour options, and helpful hints

• **Sights** with ratings:

▲▲▲—Don't miss

▲▲—Try hard to see

▲—Worthwhile if you can make it

No rating—Worth knowing about

• **Sleeping and Eating,** with good-value recommendations in every price range

• **Connections,** with tips on trains, buses, and driving

Practicalities, near the end of this book, has information on money, phoning, hotel reservations, transportation, and more.

To travel smartly, read this little book in its entirety before you go. It's my hope that this guide will make your trip more meaningful and rewarding. Traveling like a temporary local, you'll get the absolute most out of every mile, minute, and dollar.

Happy travels!

Rick Steves

NORTHERN IRELAND

NORTHERN IRELAND

 The island of Ireland was once the longest-held colony of Great Britain. Unlike its Celtic cousins, Scotland and Wales, Ireland has always been distant from London—a distance due more to its Catholicism than the Irish Sea.

Four hundred years ago, Protestant settlers from England and Scotland were strategically "planted" in Catholic Ireland to help assimilate the island into the British economy. These settlers established their own cultural toehold on the island, while the Catholic Irish held strong to their Gaelic culture.

Over the centuries, British rule hasn't been easy. By the beginning of the 20th century, the sparse Protestant population could no longer control the entire island. When Ireland won its independence in 1921 (after a bloody guerrilla war against British rule), 26 of the island's 32 counties became the Irish Free State, ruled from Dublin with dominion status in the British Commonwealth—similar to Canada's level of sovereignty. In 1949, these 26 counties left the Commonwealth and became the Republic of Ireland, severing all political ties with Britain. Meanwhile, the six remaining northeastern counties—the only ones with a Protestant majority—chose not to join the Irish Free State, and remained part of the UK.

But embedded within these six counties—now joined as the political entity called Northern Ireland—was a large, disaffected Catholic minority who felt they'd been sold down the river by the drawing of the new international border. Their political opponents were the "Unionists"—Protestants eager to defend the union with Britain, who were primarily led by two groups: the long-established Orange Order, and the military muscle of the newly mobilized Ulster Volunteer Force (UVF). This was countered on the Catholic side by the Irish Republican Army (IRA), which wanted all 32 of Ireland's counties to be united in one Irish nation—their political goals were "Nationalist."

In World War II, the Republic stayed neutral while the North enthusiastically supported the Allied cause—winning a spot close to London's heart. Derry (a.k.a. Londonderry) became an essential Allied convoy port, while Belfast lost more than 800 civilians dur-

ing four Luftwaffe bombing raids in 1941. After the war, the split between North and South seemed permanent, and Britain invested heavily in Northern Ireland to bring it solidly into the UK fold.

In the Republic of Ireland (the South), where 94 percent of the population was Catholic and only 6 percent Protestant, there was a clearly dominant majority. But in the North, at the time it was formed, Catholics were still a sizable 35 percent of the population—enough to demand attention. To maintain the status quo, Protestants considered certain forms of anti-Catholic discrimination necessary. It was this discrimination that led to the Troubles, the conflict that filled headlines from the late 1960s to the late 1990s.

Four hundred years ago (during the Reformation), this was a fight over Protestant and Catholic religious differences. But over the last century, the conflict has been not about faith, but about politics: Will Northern Ireland stay part of the UK, or become part of the Republic of Ireland? The indigenous Irish of Northern Ireland, who generally want to unite with Ireland, happen to be Catholic. The descendants of the Scottish and English settlers, who generally want to remain part of Britain, happen to be Protestant.

Northern Ireland Almanac

Official Name: Since Northern Ireland is not an independent state, there is no official country name. Some call it Ulster, while others label it the Six Counties. Population-wise, it's the smallest country of the United Kingdom (the other three are England, Wales, and Scotland).

Population: Northern Ireland's 1.8 million people are about 45 percent Protestant (mostly Presbyterian and Anglican) and 40 percent Catholic. Another 5 percent profess different religions, and 10 percent claim no religious ties. English is far and away the chief language, though Gaelic (Irish) is also spoken in staunchly Nationalist Catholic communities.

Despite the country's genetic homogeneity, the population is highly segregated along political, religious, and cultural lines. Roughly speaking, the eastern seaboard is more Unionist, Protestant, and of English-Scottish heritage, while the south and west (bordering the Republic of Ireland) are Nationalist, Catholic, and of Irish descent. Cities are often clearly divided between neighborhoods of one group or the other. Early in life, locals learn to identify the highly symbolic (and highly charged) colors, jewelry, music, names, and vocabulary that distinguish the cultural groups.

Latitude and Longitude: 54°N and 5°W. It's as far north as parts of the Alaskan panhandle.

Area: 5,400 square miles (about the size of Connecticut), constituting a sixth of the island. Northern Ireland includes 6 of the island's traditional 32 counties.

Geography: Northern Ireland is shaped roughly like a doughnut, with the UK's largest lake in the middle (Lough Neagh, 150 square miles and a prime eel fishery). The terrain comprises gently rolling hills of green grass, rising to the 2,800-foot Slieve Donard. The weather is temperate, cloudy, moist, windy, and hard to predict.

Biggest Cities: Belfast, the capital, has 300,000 residents. Half a million people—nearly one in three Northern Irish—inhabit the

Partly inspired by Martin Luther King Jr. and the civil rights movement in America in the 1960s—beamed into Irish living rooms by the new magic of television news—the Catholic minority in Northern Ireland began a nonviolent struggle to end discrimination, advocating for better jobs and housing. Extremists polarized issues, and demonstrations—also broadcast on TV news—became greater Belfast area. Derry (called Londonderry by Unionists) has 85,000 people.

Economy: Northern Ireland's economy is more closely tied to the UK than to the Republic of Ireland. Sectarian violence has held back growth, and the economy gets subsidies from the UK and the EU. Traditional agriculture (potatoes and grain) is fading fast, though modern techniques and abundant grassland make Northern Ireland a major producer of sheep, cows, and grass seed. Modern software and communications companies are replacing traditional manufacturing. Shipyards are rusty relics, and the linen industry is now threadbare; both are victims of cheaper labor available in Asia.

Currency: Northern Ireland uses not the euro, but the pound (£).

Exchange rate: £1 = about $1.60.

Government: Northern Ireland is not a self-governing nation, but is part of the UK, ruled from London by Queen Elizabeth II and Prime Minister David Cameron, and represented in Parliament by 18 elected Members of Parliament. For 50 years (1922-1972), Northern Ireland was granted a great deal of autonomy and self-governance, known as "Home Rule." The current National Assembly (108-seat Parliament)—after an ineffective decade of political logjams—has recently begun to show signs of rejuvenation.

Politics are dominated, of course, by the ongoing debate between Unionists (who want to preserve the union with the UK) and Nationalists (who want to join the Republic of Ireland). Two high-profile and controversial figures have been at opposite ends of this debate: the elderly firebrand Reverend Ian Paisley for the Unionists (who now serves in the British House of Lords); and assassination-attack survivor Gerry Adams of Sinn Fein, the political arm of the IRA (who now serves in the Republic of Ireland's parliament). In a hopeful development in the spring of 2007, the two allowed themselves to be photographed together across a negotiation table (a moment both had once sworn would never happen) as London returned control of the government to Belfast.

Flag: The official flag of Northern Ireland is the Union flag of the UK. But you'll also see the green, white, and orange Irish tricolor (waved by Nationalists) and the Northern Irish flag (white with a red cross and a red hand at its center), which is used by Unionists (see "The Red Hand of Ulster" sidebar on page 30).

violent. Unionists were afraid that if the island became one nation, the relatively poor Republic of Ireland would drag down the comparatively affluent North, and that the high percentage of Catholics would spell repression for the Protestants. As Unionist Protestants and Nationalist Catholics clashed in 1969, the British Army entered the fray. Their role, initially a peacekeeping one, gradually evolved into acting as muscle for the Unionist government. In 1972, a watershed year, more than 500 people died as combatants moved from petrol bombs to guns, and a new, more violent IRA emerged. In that 30-year (1968-1998) chapter of the struggle for an independent and united Ireland, more than 3,000 people were killed.

A 1985 agreement granted Dublin a consulting role in the Northern Ireland government. Unionists bucked this idea, and violence escalated. That same year, Belfast City Hall draped a huge, defiant banner under its dome, proclaiming, *Belfast Says No.*

In 1994, the banner came down. In the 1990s—with Ireland's membership in the EU, the growth of its economy, and the weakening of the Catholic Church's influence—the consequences of a united Ireland became slightly less threatening to the Unionists. Also in 1994, the IRA declared a cease-fire, and the Protestant Ulster Volunteer Force (UVF) followed suit.

The Nationalists wanted British troops out of Northern Ireland, while the Unionists demanded that the IRA turn in its arms. Optimists hailed the signing of a breakthrough peace plan in 1998, called the "Good Friday Accord" by Nationalists, or the "Belfast Agreement" by Unionists. This led to the release of prisoners on both sides in 2000—a highly emotional event.

Recently, additional progress has taken place on both fronts. The IRA finally "verifiably put their arms beyond use" in 2005, and backed the political peace process. In 2009, most Loyalist paramilitary groups did the same. Meanwhile, British Army surveillance towers were dismantled in 2006, and the army formally ended its 38-year-long Operation Banner campaign in 2007.

A tiny splinter group of stubborn IRA diehards (calling themselves the "Real IRA") continues to smolder. Their efforts at publicity are roundly condemned not only by hard-line Unionists, but also by former IRA leaders like government minister Martin McGuinness and his Sinn Fein party, who now prefer to pursue their Nationalist goals through the democratic process.

In 2010, the peace process was jolted forward by a surprisingly forthright apology offered by British Prime Minister David Cameron, who expressed regret for the British Army's offenses on Bloody Sunday. The apology was prompted by the Saville Report—the results of an investigation conducted by the UK government as part of the Good Friday Accord. It found that the 1972 shootings of Nationalist civil-rights marchers on Bloody Sunday by British soldiers was "unjustified" and the victims innocent (to the intense relief of the victims' families, who had fought since 1972 to clear their loved ones' names).

Major hurdles to a lasting peace persist, but the downtown checkpoints are history, and the "bomb-damage clearance sales" are over. In 2013, the G8 leaders of eight of the largest economies in the world (US President Barack Obama, Russia's President Vladimir Putin, and Germany's Chancellor Angela Merkel to name a few) chose serene, lake-splattered County Fermanagh to hold their annual summit. And today, more tourists than ever are venturing north to Belfast and Derry, and cruise-ship crowds disembark in Belfast to board charter buses that fan out to visit the Giant's Causeway and Old Bushmills Distillery.

Terminology

Ulster (one of Ireland's four ancient provinces) consists of nine counties in the northern part of the island of Ireland. Six of these make up Northern Ireland (pronounced "Norn Iron" by locals), while three counties remain part of the Republic.

Unionists—and the more hardline, working-class **Loyalists**—want the North to remain in the UK. The **Ulster Unionist Party (UUP),** the political party representing moderate Unionist views, is currently led by Mike Nesbitt (Nobel Peace Prize co-winner David Trimble led the UUP from 1995 to 2005). The **Democratic Unionist Party (DUP),** led by Peter Robinson (protégé of retired Reverend Ian Paisley), takes a harder stance in defense of Unionism. The **Ulster Volunteer Force (UVF),** the **Ulster Freedom Fighters (UFF),** and the **Ulster Defense Association (UDA)** are the Loyalist paramilitary organizations mentioned most frequently in newspapers and on spray-painted walls.

Nationalists—and the more hardline, working-class **Republicans**—want a united and independent Ireland ruled by Dublin. The **Social Democratic Labor Party (SDLP),** founded by Nobel Peace Prize co-winner John Hume and currently led by Alasdair McDonnell, is the moderate political party representing Nationalist views. **Sinn Fein** (shin fayn), led by Gerry Adams, takes a harder stance in defense of Nationalism. The **Irish Republican Army (IRA)** is the Nationalist paramilitary organization (linked with Sinn Fein) mentioned most often in the press and in graffiti.

To gain more insight into the complexity of the Troubles, see the University of Ulster's informative and evenhanded Conflict Archive at http://cain.ulst.ac.uk/index.html.

Safety

A generation ago, Northern Ireland was a sadly contorted corner of the world. On my first visit, I remember thinking that even the name of this region sounded painful ("Ulster" sounded to me like a combination of "ulcer" and "blister").

Today tourists in Northern Ireland are no longer considered courageous (or reckless). When locals spot you with a map and a lost look on your face, they're likely to ask, "Wot yer lookin fer?" in their distinctive Northern accent. They're not suspicious of you, but rather trying to help you find your way. You're safer in Belfast than in many other UK cities—and far safer, statistically, than in most major US cities. You have to look for trouble to find it here. Just don't seek out spit-and-sawdust pubs in working-class neighborhoods and spew simplistic and naive opinions about sensitive local topics.

Tourists notice the tension mainly during the "marching season" (Easter-Aug, peaking in early July). July 12—"the Twelfth"—is traditionally the most confrontational day of the year in the North, when proud Protestant Unionist Orangemen march to celebrate their Britishness and their separate identity from the Republic of Ireland (often through staunchly Nationalist Catholic neighborhoods). Lay low if you stumble onto any big Orange parades.

Northern Ireland Is a Different Country

The border is almost invisible. But when you leave the Republic of Ireland and enter Northern Ireland, you *are* crossing an international border. Although you don't have to flash your passport, you do change stamps, phone cards, and money. Gas is a little cheaper in the Republic of Ireland than in Northern Ireland (so fill up before crossing the border). Meanwhile, groceries and dental procedures are cheaper in the North (put off that root canal until you hit Belfast). These price differences create a lively daily shopping trade for those living near the border.

You won't use euros here; Northern Ireland issues its own Ulster pound, which, like the Scottish pound, is interchangeable with the English pound (€1 = about £0.80; £1 = about $1.60). Some establishments near the border may take your euros, but at a lousy exchange rate. So keep any euros for your return to the Republic, and get pounds from an ATM inside Northern Ireland instead. And if you're heading to Britain next, it's best to change your Ulster pounds into English ones (free at any bank in Northern Ireland, England, Wales, or Scotland).

BELFAST

Seventeenth-century Belfast was just a village. With the influx, or "plantation," of English and (more often) Scottish settlers, the character of the place changed. After the Scots and English were brought in—and the native Irish were subjugated—Belfast boomed, spurred by the success of the local linen, rope-making, and especially shipbuilding industries. The Industrial Revolution took root with a vengeance. While the rest of Ireland remained rural and agricultural, Belfast earned its nickname ("Old Smoke") during the time when many of the brick buildings that you'll see today were built. The year 1888 marked the birth of modern Belfast. After Queen Victoria granted city status to this boomtown of 300,000, its citizens built Belfast's centerpiece, City Hall.

Belfast is the birthplace of the *Titanic* (and many other ships that didn't sink). In 2012, to mark the 100th anniversary of the *Titanic* disaster, a modern new attraction was launched in Belfast's shipyard, telling the ill-fated ship's fascinating and tragic story. Nearby, two huge, mustard-colored cranes (built in the 1970s, and once the biggest in the world, nicknamed Samson and Goliath) rise like skyscrapers. They stand idle now, but serve as a reminder of this town's former shipbuilding might...strategic enough to be the target of four Luftwaffe bombing raids in World War II.

At the beginning of the 21st century, the peace process had begun to take root, and investments from south of the border—the Republic of Ireland—injected quiet optimism into the dejected shipyards where the *Titanic* was built. Though funding has declined, Belfast officials hope the historic Titanic Quarter will continue to attract development...and lots of tourists.

Despite the economic downturn, it feels like a new morning in

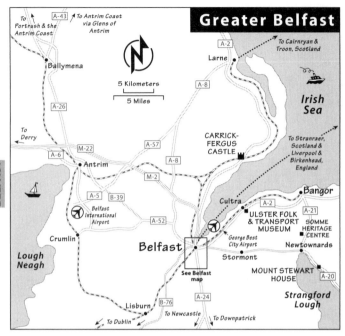

Belfast. It's hard to believe that the bright and bustling pedestrian center was once a subdued, traffic-free security zone. Now there's no hint of security checks, once a tiresome daily routine. These days, both Catholics and Protestants are rooting for the Belfast Giants ice hockey team, one of many reasons to live together peacefully.

Still, it's a fragile peace and a tenuous hope. Mean-spirited murals, hateful bonfires built a month before they're actually burned, and pubs with security gates are reminders that the island is still split—and 900,000 Protestant Unionists in the North prefer it that way.

Planning Your Time

Big Belfast is thin on sights. For most, one day of sightseeing is plenty. But I've also included advice for longer stays.

Day Trip from Dublin

Using the handy, two-hour Dublin-Belfast train (€40 "day return" tickets, €20 if booked online; can cost more Fri-Sun), you could make Belfast a day trip:

   7:35   Catch the early-morning train from Dublin's
            Connolly Station (arriving in Belfast's Central Station
            at 9:45)

11:00 City Hall tour (Mon-Fri; later on Sat, none on Sun), browse the pedestrian zone, lunch, ride a shared black taxi up Falls Road

15:00 Visit Titanic Belfast (after midday crowds subside) or side-trip to the Ulster Folk Park and Transport Museum in nearby Cultra

Evening Return to Dublin (last train departs Belfast Mon-Sat at 20:05 and arrives in Dublin at 22:15)

Sunday's trains depart later and return earlier, compressing your already limited time here (first train departs Dublin at 10:00 and arrives in Belfast at 12:16; last train departs Belfast at 19:00 and pulls into Dublin at 21:05). Confirm train times at local stations. Note that the TI offers the Historic Belfast Walk at 14:00 on Friday-Sunday (Sat-Sun only Nov-Feb). On Friday and Saturday, St. George's Market bustles in the morning. On Saturday, the only tours of City Hall are at 14:00 and 15:00. There are no tours on Sunday.

Staying Overnight

Belfast makes a pleasant overnight stop, with plenty of cheap hostels, reasonable B&Bs, weekend hotel deals (Fri-Sun), and a relaxed neighborhood full of B&Bs 30 minutes away in Bangor.

Two Days in Belfast: On the first day, follow my day-trip itinerary described earlier. For your second day, take the City Sightseeing bus tour in the morning, then visit Carrickfergus Castle in the afternoon.

Two Days in Small-Town Northern Ireland: From Dublin (via Belfast), take the train to Portrush; allow two nights and a day to tour the Causeway Coast (castle, whiskey distilleries, Giant's Causeway, resort fun), then follow the Belfast-in-a-day plan described earlier. With a third day, add Derry.

Coming from Scotland or England: With cheap flights from Edinburgh or Glasgow (check www.skyscanner.com), as well as decent but slow ferry connections (from Troon or Cairnryan in Scotland or Liverpool in England; see "Belfast Connections," later), it's easy to begin your exploration of the Emerald Isle in Belfast, and then head south to Dublin and the Republic.

Orientation to Belfast

For the first-time visitor in town for a quick look, Belfast is pretty simple. There are four zones of interest: **northern** (Titanic Quarter—docklands with Odyssey entertainment complex and Titanic Belfast), **western** (working-class sectarian neighborhoods west of the freeway), **central** (Donegall Square, City Hall, pedestrian shopping, TI), and **southern** (Botanic Gardens, Queen's University, Ulster Museum).

The modern bookends of sightseeing interest are the Titanic Belfast attraction (in the Titanic Quarter to the north) and the Lyric Theatre (near the university district to the south). Their contemporary angularities are hard to miss, as they contrast sharply with the red-brick uniformity of old Belfast. But the core of your city navigating will hinge on four more central landmarks (listed from north to south): Albert Clock Tower, City Hall, Shaftesbury Square, and Queen's University. Find them on your map, and use them to navigate as you stroll the town.

Belfast's "Golden Mile"—stretching from Hotel Europa to the university district—connects the central and southern zones with many of the best dinner and entertainment spots.

Tourist Information

The modern TI (look for *Welcome Centre* signs) has fine, free city maps and an enjoyable bookshop with Internet access (£2/hour). The *Failte Ireland* desk can answer questions about travel in the Republic of Ireland (June-Sept Mon-Sat 9:00-19:00, Sun 11:00-16:00; Oct-May Mon-Sat 9:00-17:30, Sun 11:00-16:00; one block north of City Hall at 47 Donegall Place, tel. 028/9024-6609, www.gotobelfast.com). City walking tours depart from the TI (see "Tours in Belfast," later). Be sure to pick up a free copy of *About Belfast*, which lists all the sightseeing and evening entertainment options.

Arrival in Belfast

By Train: Arriving by fast train, you'll go directly to Belfast's Central Station (with ATMs and free city maps in the lobby). From the station, a free Centrelink bus loops to Donegall Square, with stops near Shaftesbury Square (recommended hostel), the bus station (some recommended hotels), and the TI (free with any train or bus ticket, 4/hour, never on Sun; during morning rush hour, bus runs only between station and Donegall Square). Allow about £5 for a taxi from Central Station to Donegall Square, or £7 to my accommodation listings south of the university.

Slower trains arc through the city, stopping at several downtown stations, including Central Station, Great Victoria Station (most central, near Donegall Square and most hotels), and Botanic Station (close to the university, Botanic Gardens, and some recommended lodgings). It's easy and cheap to connect stations by train (£1.50).

By Car: Driving in Belfast, although not as bad as in Dublin, is still a pain. Avoid it if possible. Street parking in the city center is geared for short shopping stops (use pay-and-display machines, £0.30/15 minutes, one-hour maximum, Mon-Sat 9:00-18:00, free in evenings and on Sun).

Helpful Hints

Market: On Friday, Saturday, and Sunday (roughly until 15:00), the Victorian confines of **St. George's Market** is a commotion of commerce and a people-watching delight. Friday is a variety market, Saturday blooms with food and garden items, and Sunday creaks with crafts and antiques (at corner of Oxford and East Bridge Streets, 5 blocks east of Donegall Square, tel. 028/9043-5704, www.belfastcity.gov.uk/markets).

Shopping Mall: Victoria Square is a glitzy American-style mall. Its huge glass dome reflects Belfast's economic rejuvenation. For fine city views, ride the free elevator to the observation platform high up inside the dome (Mon-Tue 9:00-19:00, Wed-Fri 9:00-21:00, Sat 9:00-18:00, Sun 13:00-18:00; 3 blocks east of City Hall—bordered by Chichester, Victoria, Ann, and Montgomery streets; www.victoriasquare.com).

Phone Tips: To call the Republic of Ireland from Northern Ireland, dial 00-353, then the area code without its initial 0, and finally the local number. To call Northern Ireland from the Republic of Ireland, dial 048, and then the local eight-digit number.

Internet Access: Belfast's Internet cafés are here-today, gone-tomorrow ventures operating on a shoestring. The **TI** offers dependable Internet access at a half-dozen handy terminals (£2/hour). There's Wi-Fi at the Student Union, listed below.

Post Office: The main post office, with lots of fun postcards, is at the intersection of High and Bridge Streets (Mon-Fri 9:00-17:30, Sat 9:00-12:30, closed Sun, 3 long blocks north of Donegall Square). A second branch is located across from the Ulster Museum, and a third location lurks north of City Hall, at the corner of High and North Streets (all same hours).

Laundry: Globe Launderers is at 37-39 Botanic Avenue (£5 self-serve, £8 drop-off service, Mon-Fri 8:00-21:00, Sat 8:00-18:00, Sun 12:00-18:00, tel. 028/9024-3956). For the hotel neighborhood south of the university, the closest is **Whistle Cleaners** (£8 drop-off service, Mon-Fri 8:30-18:00, Sat 9:00-17:30, closed Sun, 160 Lisburn Road, at intersection with Eglantine Avenue, tel. 028/9038-1297).

Bike Rental: Belfast Bike Tours rents bikes only if reserved in advance (£15/day, daily but no set hours, off Wellington Park

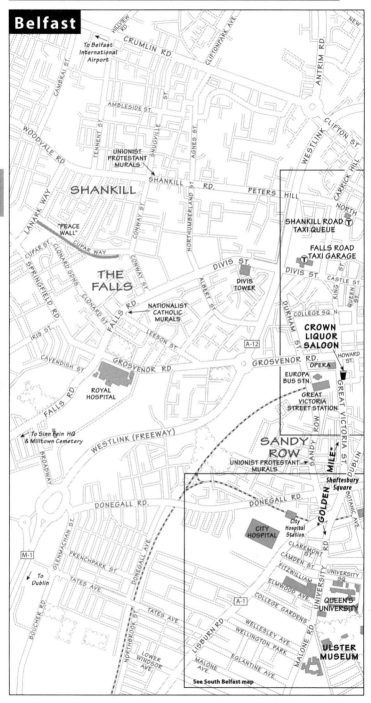

Belfast

To Belfast International Airport

CRUMLIN RD.
HILLVIEW RD.
CLIFTONPARK AVE.
NEW
ANTRIM RD.
CAMBRAI ST.
AMBLESIDE ST.
CLIFTON ST.
WOODVALE RD.
TENNENT ST.
SNUGVILLE ST.
AGNES ST.
WESTLINK
CARRICK HILL

UNIONIST PROTESTANT MURALS

SHANKILL
SHANKILL RD.
PETERS HILL
NORTH

"PEACE WALL"
LANARK WAY
CUPAR WAY
CONWAY ST.
NORTHUMBERLAND ST.

SHANKILL ROAD TAXI QUEUE

CUPAR ST.
CLONARD GDNS.
SPRINGFIELD RD.
CLONARD ST.
FALLS RD.
ALBERT ST.
DIVIS ST.
DIVIS TOWER

FALLS ROAD TAXI GARAGE

DIVIS ST.
CASTLE ST.
KING ST.
QUEEN ST.

THE FALLS

NATIONALIST CATHOLIC MURALS

LEESON ST.
COLLEGE SQ. N

CROWN LIQUOR SALOON

IRIS ST.
CAVENDISH ST.
A-12

GROSVENOR RD.
GROSVENOR RD.
HOWARD ST.
OPERA

ROYAL HOSPITAL

DURHAM ST.

EUROPA BUS STN.

To Sinn Fein HQ & Milltown Cemetery

GREAT VICTORIA STREET STATION

FALLS RD.
WESTLINK (FREEWAY)

GREAT VICTORIA ST.
DUBLIN RD.

SANDY ROW

UNIONIST PROTESTANT MURALS
SANDY ROW
"GOLDEN MILE"
Shaftesbury Square
BOTANIC AVE.

BROADWAY
DONEGALL RD.
DONEGALL RD.

CITY HOSPITAL
City Hospital Station

CLAREMONT ST.
CAMDEN ST.
FITZWILLIAM
ELMWOOD AVE.
UNIVERSITY RD.
UNIVERSITY SQ.

M-1
GLENMACHAN ST.
FRENCHPARK ST.
DONEGALL AVE.

To Dublin
TATES AVE.
COLLEGE GARDENS
QUEEN'S UNIVERSITY

BOUCHER RD.
TATES AVE.
A-1
LISBURN RD.
WELLESLEY AVE.
WELLINGTON PARK
MALONE RD.
ULSTER MUSEUM

NORTHBROOK ST.
LOWER WINDSOR AVE.
MALONE RD.
EGLANTINE AVE.

See South Belfast map

BELFAST

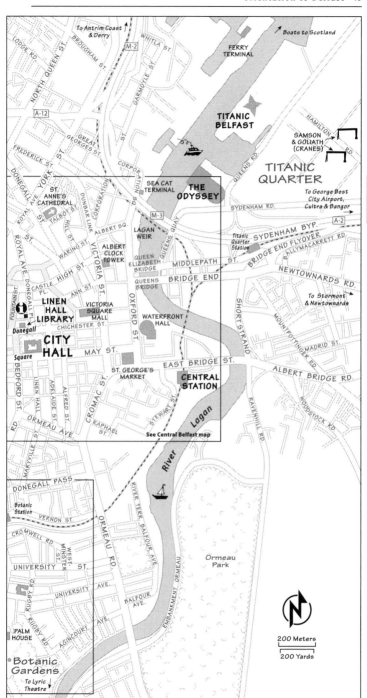

To Antrim Coast & Derry
Boats to Scotland
FERRY TERMINAL
M-2
WHITLA ST.
BROUGHAM ST.
GARMOYLE ST.
NORTH QUEEN ST.
LODGE RD.
GREAT GEORGES ST.
ST.
A-12
FREDERICK ST.
CORPORATION ST.
TITANIC BELFAST
HAMILTON RD.
QUEENS RD.
SAMSON & GOLIATH (CRANES)
TITANIC QUARTER
DONEGALL ST.
ROYAL AVE.
YORK ST.
ST. ANNE'S CATHEDRAL
TALBOT ST.
DUNBAR LINK
ALBERT SQ.
SEA CAT TERMINAL
THE ODYSSEY
To George Best City Airport, Cultra & Bangor
SYDENHAM RD.
A-2
M-3
LAGAN WEIR
QUEENS QUAY
WARING ST.
HIGH ST.
ALBERT CLOCK TOWER
VICTORIA ST.
QUEEN ELIZABETH BRIDGE
MIDDLEPATH ST.
Titanic Quarter Station
SYDENHAM BYP.
BRIDGE END FLYOVER
BALLYMACARRETT RD.
CASTLE PL.
HIGH ST.
DONEGALL PL.
FOUNTAIN ST.
ANN ST.
QUEENS BRIDGE
BRIDGE END
NEWTOWNARDS RD.
LINEN HALL LIBRARY
VICTORIA SQUARE MALL
OXFORD ST.
MOUNTPOTTINGER RD.
MADRID ST.
To Stormont & Newtownards
Donegall Square
CITY HALL
CHICHESTER ST.
WATERFRONT HALL
SHORT STRAND
BEDFORD ST.
MAY ST.
ALBERT BRIDGE RD.
LINEN HALL ST.
ADELAIDE ST.
ALFRED ST.
CROMAC ST.
ST. GEORGE'S MARKET
EAST BRIDGE ST.
CENTRAL STATION
RAVENHILL RD.
WOODSTOCK RD.
ORMEAU AVE.
MARYVILLE ST.
RAPHAEL ST.
STEWART ST.
River Lagan
See Central Belfast map
DONEGALL PASS
Botanic Station
VERNON ST.
RIVER TERR.
BALFOUR AVE.
ORMEAU RD.
CROMWELL RD.
WESTMINSTER ST.
UNIVERSITY
UNIVERSITY AVE.
RUGBY RD.
RUGBY AVE.
AGINCOURT AVE.
BALFOUR AVE.
EMBANKMENT ORMEAU
Ormeau Park
PALM HOUSE
Botanic Gardens
To Lyric Theatre

N

200 Meters
200 Yards

behind Wellington Park Hotel, mobile 078-1211-4235, www.belfastbiketours.com).

Queen's University Student Union: Located directly across University Road from the red-brick university building, the Student Union is just as handy for tourists as it is for college students. Inside you'll find an ATM (at end of main hall, on the right), WCs, a pharmacy, a mini-market, and Wi-Fi. Grab a quick and cheap £4 sandwich and coffee at **Clement's Coffee Shop** (Mon-Fri 8:30-22:30, Sat 9:00-22:00, closed Sun).

Updates to This Book: For updates to this book, check www.ricksteves.com/update.

Getting Around Belfast

If you line up your sightseeing logically, you can do most of the town on foot. On wheels, you have several options.

By Train or Bus: Ask about iLink smartcards, which give individuals one day of unlimited train and bus travel. The Zone 1 card (£6.50) covers the city center and George Best Belfast City Airport. The handy Zone 2 card (£10.50) includes Cultra (Ulster Folk Park and Transport Museum), Bangor, and Carrickfergus Castle. The Zone 3 card (£14) is really only useful for reaching Belfast's distant airport or the Ulster American Folk Park near Omagh. Zone 4 (£16.50) gets you anywhere in Northern Ireland, including Portrush and Derry. You can purchase additional iLink days to top up your card (£5 for Zone 1, £9 for Zone 2, £12.50 for Zone 3, £15 for Zone 4). For those lingering in the North, one-week cards offer even better deals. Buy your iLink card at any train station in the city.

If you're only traveling from Belfast to one destination—Carrickfergus Castle, Cultra, or Bangor—a "day return" ticket is cheaper than two one-way tickets.

Buses go from Donegall Square East to Malone Road and my recommended accommodations (#8B or #8C, 3/hour, £1.80, all-day pass costs £4 Mon-Sat before 9:30—after 9:30 and on Sun it's £3). Sunday service is much less frequent.

For information on trains and buses in Belfast, contact Translink (tel. 028/9066-6630, www.translink.co.uk).

By Taxi: Taxis are reasonable and a good option. For general transport, as opposed to the taxi tours described later, try **Valu Cabs** (tel. 028/9080-9080). Rather than use their meters, many cabs charge a flat £5 rate for any ride up to two miles. It's £2 per mile after that. If you're going up Falls Road, ride a shared cab (explained later, under "Sights in Belfast").

Tours in Belfast

▲Walking Tours

The **Historic Belfast Walk** takes you through the historic core of town (£8, 1.5 hours; departs from TI March-Oct Fri-Sun at 14:00; Nov-Feb Sat and Sun only; confirm tour times with TI, book in advance, tel. 028/9024-6609).

Mixing drinks and history, **Historical Pub Tours of Belfast** offers two-hour walking tours that start at the Crown Dining Room pub and end five pubs later (£8; May-Oct Thu at 19:00, Sat at 16:00; book in advance, meet at pub above Crown Liquor Saloon at 46 Great Victoria Street across from Hotel Europa, tel. 028/9268-3665, www.belfastpubtours.com).

Coiste Irish Political Tours leads extended, three-hour walks along Falls Road to explain the history of the neighborhood from an intensely Republican perspective. Led by former IRA prisoners, you'll visit murals, gardens of remembrance, peace walls, and community centers in this rejuvenating section of gritty Belfast. Tours meet beside the Divis Tower (the 20-story apartment house at the east end of the Divis Road near the A-12 Westlink motorway overpass) and end at the Milltown Cemetery (£10, Mon-Sat at 11:00, Sun at 14:00, tel. 028/9020-0770, www.coiste.ie, Seamus Kelley). They also offer tours on United Irishmen, Ballymurphy, or Milltown Cemetery.

▲Big Bus Tours

City Sightseeing offers the best quick introduction to the city's recent and complicated political and social history. Take their bus tour to use as a handy all-day transportation service to link major sights. You'll cruise the Catholic and Protestant working-class neighborhoods, politically charged sites like the dramatically situated Stormont Parliament building and sobering Crumlin Road Gaol, and historic stops such as Titanic Belfast and City Hall. The commentary points out political murals and places of interest—often dealing with the Troubles of the last 45 years. You see sights from the bus and can get on and off at any of the stops; buses pass every half-hour (£12.50, 2/hour, daily 10:00-16:30, tickets valid for 48 hours, fewer tours in winter—call first, makes 20 stops over a 1.5-hour loop; departs from Castle Place on High Street, 2 blocks west of Albert Clock Tower; pay cash on bus, or book by phone with credit card, tel. 028/9045-9035, www.city-sightseeing.com).

Their cousin tour is the **Titanic Explorer** hop-on, hop-off bus, which focuses only on the Titanic Quarter. Stops lace together the Odyssey, S.S. *Nomadic* tender ship, Titanic Belfast, and Harland and Wolff drawing offices, and include a brief guided tour of *Titanic*'s Dry Dock and Pump-House (£10, hourly, daily 9:45-16:00, ticket valid 24 hours, fewer in winter—call first, makes eight stops over 45-minute loop; departs from Castle Place on High Street, 2 blocks west of Albert Clock Tower, pay cash on bus, or book by phone with credit card, tel. 028/9032-1321, www.titanicexplorer. com).

Bike Tours

Explore the countryside south of town on **Belfast Bike Tours.** Departing from the front gate of Queen's University, you'll spend 2.5 hours peddling along an old canal towpath to the Giant's Ring (ancient dolmen) and back on generally flat terrain (£15; April-Aug Mon, Wed, Fri-Sat at 10:30 and 14:00; Sept-March Sat 10:30 and 14:00; bikes, helmets, and bottle of water provided; must reserve ahead by phone or email, mobile 078-1211-4235, www.belfastbiketours.com).

Minibus Tours

McComb's Giant's Causeway Tour visits Carrickfergus Castle, the Giant's Causeway, Dunluce Castle (photo stop only), Carrick-a-Rede Rope Bridge, and Old Bushmills Distillery (£25, doesn't include distillery admission, daily 9:15-18:45 depending on demand, book through and depart from the recommended Belfast International City Hostel, 9:15 pickup at hostel, 9:45 pickup at Hilton Hotel—a block north of Central Station). They also have private guides (book in advance, tel. 028/9031-5333, www.mccombscoaches.com).

Boat Tours

The Lagan Boat Company shows you shipyards on a one-hour **Titanic Tour** cruise, narrated by a member of the Belfast Titanic

Society. The tour shows off the fruits of the city's £800 million investment in its harbor, including a weir built to control the tides and stabilize the depth of the harbor (it doubles as a free pedestrian bridge over the River Lagan). The heart of the tour is a lazy harbor cruise past rusty dry-dock gates, brought alive by the guide's proud commentary and passed-around historical photos (£10; April-Oct daily sailings at 12:30, 14:00, and 15:30; fewer off-season, tel. 028/9033-0844, mobile 077-1891-0423, www.laganboatcompany.com). Tours depart from the Lagan Pedestrian Bridge and Weir on Donegall Quay. The quay is located just past the leaning Albert Clock Tower, a five-minute walk from the TI.

Local Guide

Ken Harper has a vast knowledge of Belfast and does insightful tours from his taxi, focusing on both Catholic and Protestant neighborhoods, *Titanic*-related sights, and Belfast's favorite sons—author C. S. Lewis, musician Van Morrison, and soccer star/playboy George Best. He's also available for custom tours, which he calls "Pick Ken's Brain" (£30 minimum or £10/person, 1.25 hours, tel. 028/9074-2711, mobile 077-1175-7178, www.harpertaxitours.com, kenharper2004@hotmail.com).

Sights in Belfast

Most sights of interest are located in four areas: the Titanic Quarter to the north of the city center, the sectarian neighborhoods to the west of the city center, central Belfast, and south Belfast (clustered around Queen's University).

Titanic Quarter

Up until the mid-1990s, this district was a barren wasteland of cement slabs and rusting industrial relics. But during the Celtic Tiger boom years (which spilled over into the North), shrewd investors saw the real-estate potential and began building posh, high-rise condos.

The first landmark project to be completed was the Odyssey entertainment complex (in 2000). To draw more visitors and commemorate the proud shipbuilding industry of the Victorian and Edwardian Ages, another flagship attraction was needed. The 100th anniversary of the *Titanic* disaster in 2012 provided the perfect opportunity, and the result is a brand-new attraction called Titanic Belfast.

The Odyssey

This huge millennium-project complex offers a food pavilion, bowling alley, and W5 science center with interactive, educational exhibits for youngsters. Where else can a kid play a harp with laser-light strings? The "W5" stands for "who, what, when, where, and why" (£7.90, kids-£5.90, Mon-Fri 10:00-17:00, Sat 10:00-18:00, Sun 12:00-18:00, 2 Queen's Quay, 10-minute walk north of Belfast's Central Station, tel. 028/9046-7790, www.w5online.co.uk). There's also a 12-screen cinema, laser-tag gaming area, and an 8,000-seat arena where the Belfast Giants professional ice hockey team skates from September to March on Friday or Saturday nights (£15 game tickets, tel. 028/9073-9074, www.belfastgiants.com).

▲▲▲Titanic Belfast

This £97 million attraction sits on the site of the original dry dock where the ship was built. High-tech displays tell the tale of the famous cruise

BELFAST

Titanic Trio

Most of us already know the sad story of the famous *Titanic,* when the unthinkable happened to the unsinkable: Launched in Belfast in 1911, the *Titanic* was the largest and most celebrated luxury cruise liner of its time.

Locals thought themselves the best shipbuilders since Noah. The Titanic's sudden demise in 1912 is the most famous sea disaster of the modern era. Only 716 of the 2,260 aboard were rescued; 70 percent of the first-class passengers, with first dibs on the few lifeboats, survived.

While everyone has heard of the *Titanic,* few people know that it was the middle sister of three unfortunate ships, each built in Belfast by the prestigious Harland and Wolff shipyards for the White Star Line.

In 1910, the **Olympic** was the first of the three similar vessels to be launched. It soon collided with the naval cruiser HMS *Hawke* and returned to Belfast to be repaired with parts taken from the still-under-construction **Titanic.** When World War I began, the *Olympic* served as a troop transport ship. During the war, it struck and sank a German submarine (the U-103). After the war, it returned to commercial service and later collided with the *Nantucket Lightship* (killing seven). The *Olympic*'s last voyage was in 1935, and it was demolished in 1937.

The last of the three to be built was the **Gigantic** in 1914. But after the *Titanic* sank, its name was changed (while still under construction) to **Britannic**...which was thought to be a luckier name. It was repainted white and converted to a hospital ship at the start of World War I. In 1915, it was serving in the Aegean Sea when it hit a mine—or was struck by a torpedo from a U-boat. Fortunately it had more advanced safety features than its two older sisters—it had enough lifeboats for all onboard, and was designed to sink more slowly. Luckily, the ship had no patients yet, as it was on its way to Greece to pick up wounded soldiers. Most of those onboard were saved (only 30 of the almost 1,100 crew and medical staff died). In 1976, French underwater explorer Jacques Cousteau found the wreck of the *Britannic* 400 feet down and brought up a few of its artifacts.

Amazingly, a single human thread ties all three ships together. A stewardess and nurse named Violet Jessop was aboard the *Olympic* when it collided with the HMS *Hawke*. She was also one of the lucky few to be rescued from the *Titanic*. And yes, incredibly, she was again among those rescued from the sinking *Britannic*. Talk about a buoyant personality...

liner, proudly heralded as the largest man-made moving object of its time.

Cost and Hours: £14.75, £18.25 combo-ticket with Dry Dock and Pump-House (described later), audioguide for infoholics—£3, daily April-Sept 9:00-19:00, Oct-March 10:00-17:00, located where the famous ship was built on Queen's Island, tel. 028/9076-6399, www.titanicbelfast.com.

Crowd-Beating Tips: This attraction drew 800,000 visitors in its first year (double what was expected). Go early or late; big bus-tour crowds clog the exhibits from 10:00 to 14:00. Book ahead online to ensure the entry time you want.

Eating: The ground floor includes a sandwich café as well as a carvery-style restaurant.

Getting There: From Donegall Square, take bus #26 or #26B (both stop behind Belfast Metropolitan College, a block away from Donegall Square; infrequent buses on Sun), or go by taxi (£6 ride). The Titanic Quarter train station is a 10-minute walk to the south of the Titanic Belfast. The Dry Dock and Pump-House (described later) are another 10-minute walk north of the Titanic Belfast.

Visiting the Titanic Belfast: The spacey architecture of Titanic Belfast's new building is already a landmark on the city's skyline. Six stories tall, it's clad in over 3,000 sun-reflecting aluminum panels. Its four corners represent the bows of the many ships that were built in these yards during the golden age of Belfast.

Inside, nine galleries take you from booming 1900s Belfast, through the construction and launch of the *Titanic,* and ultimately to a re-creation of its watery grave. A highlight is the Shipyard Ride, which takes you through a mock-up of the ship while it was being built. You'll learn how workers toughed out months of deafening and dangerous duty, working in five-man teams to hammer in red-hot rivets (they were paid by the rivet, and were frequently burned by chips flying off the metal). For efficiency, left- and right-handers were assigned specific hammering positions. Young boys had the hot and hazardous job of quickly catching the glowing rivets and placing them for the hammerers.

Other exhibits cover the wider story of the Harland and Wolff shipyards, including the construction of *Titanic's* lesser-known and also ill-fated sister ships: *Olympic* and *Britannic* (see sidebar). An upper-floor viewpoint employs innovative electronic windows to project an image of the huge, partially built *Titanic* in dry dock beside you, masking the reality of today's barren shipyard below. Another gallery surrounds you on three sides with animated screens that glide through multiple decks, giving you a realistic feel for the ship in all its full-steam-ahead glory.

The human story of its passengers—from promenade-deck aristocrats to heroic crew members to steerage-class rabble—is also here. The passenger manifest encompassed virtually every segment of society: In today's dollars, a first-class ticket would cost $70,000, while a third-class ticket would cost $650. You'll see a broad cross-section of displays from the ship's short but opulent existence.

The big-screen "Titanic Beneath" theater shows the now-famous underwater footage of the wreck nearly 12,500 feet down on the ocean floor. Only 20 percent of the dead were ever recovered. Don't miss the see-through floor panels at the foot of the movie screen, which allow you to stand on top of the watery debris field as the virtual wreck slowly passes beneath your feet.

Dry Dock and Pump-House

Those with an unsinkable interest in the *Titanic* may want to walk down into the massive footprint where it last rested on dry land, to get a feel for how colossal the vessel was. Personally, I'd skip the entry cost and just take in the free view down into the dock from behind the fence.

Cost and Hours: £6, or £1 more for tour, also covered by £18.25 combo-ticket with Titanic Belfast, daily 10:00-17:00, www.titanicsdock.com.

Getting There: From the Titanic Belfast, it's a 300-yard walk to the Dry Dock and Pump-House. En route, you'll pass the massive **Titanic Studios** building, where parts of *Game of Thrones* and *City of Ember* were filmed.

Sectarian Neighborhoods in West Belfast

It will be a happy day when the sectarian neighborhoods of Belfast have nothing to be sectarian about. For a look at three of the original home bases of the Troubles, explore the working-class neighborhoods of Catholic Falls Road and Protestant Shankill Road (west of the Westlink motorway), or Protestant Sandy Row (south of the Westlink motorway).

Murals (found in working-class, sectarian areas) are a memorable part of any visit to Belfast. But with more peaceful times, the character of these murals is slowly changing. The Re-Imaging Communities Program has spent £3 million in government money to replace aggressive murals with positive ones. Paramilitary themes are gradually being covered over with images of pride in each neighborhood's culture. The *Titanic* was built primarily by proud Protestant Ulster stock and is often seen in their neighborhood murals—reflecting their industrious work ethic. Over in the Catholic neighborhoods, you'll see more murals depicting mythological heroes from the days before the English came.

You can get taxi tours of Falls Road or Shankill Road (see next listings), but rarely are both combined well in one tour. Ken Harper is one of a new breed of Belfast taxi drivers who will give you an insightful private tour of both neighborhoods (for contact info, see "Tours in Belfast—Local Guide," earlier).

▲▲Falls Road (Catholic)

At the intersection of Castle and King Streets, you'll find the Castle Junction Car Park. On the ground floor of this nine-story

parking garage, a passenger terminal (entrance on King Street) connects travelers with old black cabs—and the only Irish-language signs in downtown Belfast. These shared black cabs efficiently shuttle residents from outlying neighborhoods up and down Falls Road and to the city center. This service originated more than 40 years ago at the beginning of the Troubles, when locals would hijack city buses and use them as barricades in the street fighting. When bus service was discontinued, local paramilitary groups established the shared taxi service. Although the buses are now running again, these cab rides are still a great value for their drivers' commentary.

Any cab goes up Falls Road, past Sinn Fein headquarters and lots of murals, to the Milltown Cemetery (£6, sit in front and talk to the cabbie). Hop in and out. Easy-to-flag-down cabs run every minute or so in each direction on Falls Road.

Forty trained cabbies do one-hour tours (minimum £30, £10/person for 1.5 hours, £20/additional hour, cheap for a small group of up to 6 riders, tel. 028/9031-5777 or mobile 078-9271-6660, www.taxitrax.com).

The Sinn Fein office and bookstore are near the bottom of Falls Road. The **bookstore** is worth a look. Page through books featuring color photos of the political murals that decorated these buildings. Money raised here supports the families of deceased IRA members.

A sad, corrugated structure called the **Peace Wall** runs a block or so north of Falls Road (along Cupar Way), separating the Catholics from the Protestants in the Shankill Road area. The first cement wall was 20 feet high—it was later extended another 10 feet by a solid metal addition, and then another 15 feet with a metal screen. Seemingly high enough now to deter a projectile being lobbed over, this is just one of 17 such walls in Belfast.

At the **Milltown Cemetery,** walk past all the Gaelic crosses down to the far right-hand corner (closest to the highway), where the IRA Roll of Honor is set apart from the thousands of other graves by little green railings. They are treated like fallen soldiers. Notice the memorial to Bobby Sands and nine other hunger strikers. They starved themselves to death in the nearby Maze Prison in 1981, protesting for political prisoner status as opposed to terrorist criminal treatment. Maze Prison closed in the fall of 2000.

Shankill Road and Sandy Row (Protestant)

You can ride a shared black cab through the Protestant **Shankill Road** area (£30/1-2 people for one hour, £40/3-6 people, tel. 028/9032-8775). They depart from North Street near the intersection with Millfield Road; it's not well-marked, but watch where the cabs circle and pick up locals on the south side of the street.

An easier (and cheaper) way to get a dose of the Unionist side is to walk **Sandy Row.** From Hotel Europa, walk a block down Glengall Street, then turn left for a 10-minute walk along a working-class Protestant street. A stop in a Unionist memorabilia shop, a pub, or one of the many cheap eateries here may give you an opportunity to talk to a local. You'll see murals filled with Unionist symbolism. The mural of William of Orange's victory over the Catholic King James II (Battle of the Boyne, 1690) thrills Unionist hearts.

Central Belfast

▲▲City Hall

This grand structure's 173-foot-tall copper dome dominates the town center. Built between 1898 and 1906, with its statue of Queen Victoria scowling down Belfast's main drag and the Union Jack flapping behind her, the City Hall is a stirring sight. In the garden, you'll find memorials to the *Titanic* and the landing of the US Expeditionary Force in 1942—the first American troops to arrive in Europe en route to Berlin.

Take the worthwhile and free 45-minute tour, which gives you a rundown on city government and an explanation of the decor

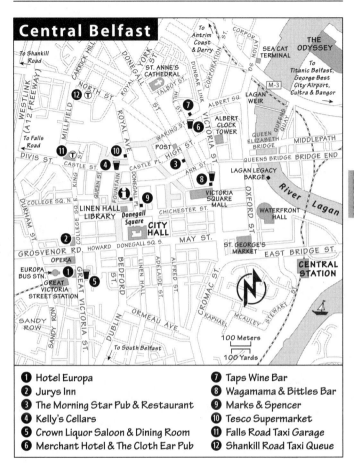

❶ Hotel Europa		❼ Taps Wine Bar	
❷ Jurys Inn		❽ Wagamama & Bittles Bar	
❸ The Morning Star Pub & Restaurant		❾ Marks & Spencer	
❹ Kelly's Cellars		❿ Tesco Supermarket	
❺ Crown Liquor Saloon & Dining Room		⓫ Falls Road Taxi Garage	
❻ Merchant Hotel & The Cloth Ear Pub		⓬ Shankill Road Taxi Queue	

that makes this an Ulster political hall of fame. Queen Victoria and King Edward VII look down on city council meetings. The 1613 original charter of Belfast granted by James I is on display. Its Great Hall—bombed by the Germans in 1941—looks as great as it did the day it was made.

Cost and Hours: Free; building open Mon-Thu 8:30-17:00, Fri 8:30-16:30, closed (except for tours) Sat, closed Sun; tours Mon-Fri at 11:00, 14:00, and 15:00—entrance on north side of building behind Queen Victoria statue; Sat at 14:00 and 15:00—entrance via south-facing back door only; no tours on Sun; call to confirm schedule and to reserve a tour, handy Bobbin coffee shop on ground floor, tel. 028/9032-0202, www.belfastcity.gov.uk/cityhall.

Visiting City Hall on Your Own: If you can't manage a tour, at least step inside to admire the marble swirl staircase and the

BELFAST

1916

This pivotal year means vastly different things to Northern Ireland's two communities. When you say "1776" to most Americans, it means revolution and independence from tyranny (unless, perhaps, you're a Native American). But when you say "1916" to someone in Northern Ireland, the response depends on who's talking.

To Nationalists (who are usually Catholic), "1916" brings to mind the Easter Uprising—which took place in Dublin in April of that year and was the beginning of the end of 750 years of British rule for most of Ireland. Some Nationalist murals still use images of Dublin's rebel headquarters or martyred leaders like Patrick Pearse and James Connolly. To this community, 1916 emphasizes their proud Gaelic identity, their willingness to fight to preserve it, and their stubborn anti-British attitude.

To Unionists (who are usually Protestant), "1916" means the brutal WWI Battle of

view up into the dome. In 1912, at the center of the marble floor design beneath the dome, Sir Edward Carson signed the Ulster Covenant—to be followed by 470,000 other Unionists at dozens of desks surrounding City Hall that day. Some signed with their own blood. The Covenant stated Unionists would use "all means necessary" (including the might of the 100,000-strong UVF militia) to resist the Home Rule bill that had just passed in Parliament. The bill would have given the island of Ireland limited autonomy from Britain. These Protestant Unionists feared "Home Rule as Rome Rule," where they would have become the minority in an independent Catholic Ireland. World War I interrupted the implementation of Home Rule, and the partition of Ireland followed shortly after the war's end.

Linen Hall Library

Across the street from City Hall, the 200-year-old Linen Hall Library welcomes guests (notice the red hand above the former front door facing Donegall Square North). Described as "Ulster's attic," the library takes pride in being a neutral space where anyone trying to make sense of the sectarian conflict can view the Troubled Images, a historical collection of engrossing political posters. It has a fine hardbound ambience, a coffee shop, and a royal newspaper reading room.

Cost and Hours: Free, Mon-Fri 9:30-17:30, Sat 9:30-16:00, the Somme in France, which began that July. (For more on the Somme, visit the Somme Heritage Centre in Bangor, described on page 42.) Although both Catholic and Protestant soldiers died in this long and bloody battle, the first wave of young men who went over the top were the sons of proud Ulster Unionists. The

Unionists hoped this sacrifice would prove their loyalty to the Crown—and assurance that the British would never let them be gobbled up by an Irish Nationalist state (a possible scenario just before the Great War's outbreak). You'll see Tommies heroically climbing out of their trenches in some of Belfast's Unionist murals. For the Unionists, 1916 is synonymous with devout, almost righteously divine, Britishness.

It will be interesting to see how the people of Northern Ireland choose to celebrate the 100th anniversary of 1916...coming up in the not-so-distant future.

closed Sun, entrance on Fountain Street, 17 Donegall Square North, tel. 028/9032-1707, www.linenhall.com.

Golden Mile

This is the overstated nickname of Belfast's liveliest dining and entertainment district, which stretches from the Opera House (Great Victoria Street) to the university (University Road).

The **Grand Opera House,** originally built in 1895, bombed and rebuilt in 1991, and bombed and rebuilt again in 1993, is extravagantly Victorian and *the* place to take in a concert, play, or opera (ticket office open Mon-Fri 9:30-17:30, Sat 12:00-17:00, closed Sun; ticket office to right of main front door on Great Victoria Street, tel. 028/9024-1919, www.goh.co.uk). The recommended **Hotel Europa,** next door, while considered to be the most-bombed hotel in the world, actually feels pretty casual (but is expensive to stay in).

Across the street is the museum-like **Crown Liquor Saloon.** Built in 1849, it's now a part of the National Trust. A wander through its mahogany, glass, and marble interior is a trip back into the days of Queen Victoria, although the privacy provided by the snugs—booths—allows for un-Victorian behavior (Mon-Sat 11:30-24:00, Sun 12:30-23:00, consider a lunch stop—see listing under "Eating in Belfast," later). Upstairs, the Crown Dining Room serves pub grub, is decorated with historic photos, and is the starting point for a pub walk (listed earlier, under "Tours in Belfast").

Lagan Legacy

Housed in the barge MV *Confiance*, docked on the west bank of the Lagan River, this museum bridges the gap between the Ulster Museum's eclectic displays and Titanic Belfast's modern pizazz. More of a city museum for Belfast, the exhibits here were donated by locals who valued the preservation of their proud industrial and maritime heritage. A visit starts with an interesting 30-minute film giving a good overview of city history. You're then free to wander the hold of the ship, exploring interactive displays about the lives of average workers as well as models of industrial innovations like the huge Harland and Wolff cranes and Belfast-built oil rigs. The museum proclaims that the story of Belfast is "the greatest story never told."

Cost and Hours: £4, daily 10:00-16:00, coffee shop on main deck, at Lanyon Quay just south of Queen's Bridge, tel. 028/9023-2555, www.belfastbarge.com.

South Belfast

▲Ulster Museum

While mediocre by European standards, this is Belfast's most venerable museum. It offers an earnest and occasionally thought-provoking look at a cross-section of local artifacts.

Cost and Hours: Free, Tue-Sun 10:00-17:00, closed Mon, in Botanic Gardens on Stranmillis Road, south of downtown, tel. 028/9044-0000, www.nmni.com.

Visiting the Museum: The four-floor museum is free and pretty painless. Ride the elevator to the top floor and follow the spiraling exhibits downhill through various zones. The top floor is dedicated to rotating art exhibits, the next floor down covers local nature, and the one below that focuses on history. The ground floor covers the modern Troubles, and has a coffee shop and gift shop.

The Art Zone displays a beautifully crafted Belleek vase, as well as fine crystal and china. In the Nature Zone, audiovisuals trace how the Ice Age affected the local landscape. Dinosaur skeletons lurk, stuffed wildlife plays possum, and geology rocks. Kids will enjoy the interactive Discover History room.

The delicately worded History Zone has an interesting British slant (such as the implication that most deaths in the Great Potato Famine of 1845-1849 were caused by typhus and fever epidemics—without mentioning the starvation that made peasants susceptible to these diseases in the first place). But the coverage of the modern-day Troubles is balanced and thought-provoking.

After a peek at a pretty good mummy, top things off with the *Girona* treasure. Soggy bits of gold, silver, leather, and wood were salvaged from the Spanish Armada's shipwrecked *Girona*, lost off the Antrim Coast north of Belfast in 1588.

▲Botanic Gardens

This is the backyard of Queen's University, and on a sunny day, you couldn't imagine a more relaxing park setting. On a cold day, step into the Tropical Ravine for a jungle of heat and humidity. Take a quick walk through the Palm House, reminiscent of the one in London's Kew Gardens, but smaller. The Ulster Museum is on the garden's grounds.

Cost and Hours: Free, gardens open daily 8:00 until dusk; Palm House open Mon-Fri 10:00-12:00 & 13:00-17:00, Sat-Sun 13:00-17:00, shorter hours in winter; tel. 028/9031-4762, www.belfastcity.gov.uk/parks.

Lyric Theatre

Rebuilt in 2011, this Belfast institution represents the cultural rejuvenation of the city. It's located beside the Lagan River (near Queen's University) in an architecturally innovative building partially funded by donations from famous actors such as Liam Neeson, Kenneth Branagh, and Meryl Streep. While there are no public tours, it's a good place to see quality local productions (tickets-£15-25; box office open Mon-Sat 10:00-17:00, closed Sun; 55 Ridgeway Street, tel. 028/9038-1081, www.lyrictheatre.co.uk).

Near Belfast

▲▲Ulster Folk Park and Transport Museum

This sprawling 180-acre, two-museum complex straddles the road and rail line at Cultra, midway between Bangor and Belfast (8 miles east of town).

Cost and Hours: £7.50 for Folk Park, £7.50 for Transport Museum, £9 combo-ticket for both, £24.50 for families; March-Sept Tue-Sun 10:00-17:00; Oct-Feb Tue-Fri 10:00-16:00, Sat-Sun 11:00-16:00; closed Mon year-round; check the schedule for the day's special events, tel. 028/9042-8428, www.nmni.com.

Getting There: From Belfast, you can reach Cultra by taxi (£15), bus #502 (2/hour, 30 minutes, from Laganside Bus Centre), or train (£5.40 round-trip, 2/hour, 15 minutes, from any Belfast train station or from Bangor). Trains and buses stop right in the park, but train service is more dependable. Public-transport schedules are skimpy on Saturday and Sunday.

Planning Your Time: Allow three hours for your visit, and expect lots of walking. Most people will spend an hour in the Transport Museum and a couple of hours at the Folk Park. You'll arrive (by rail or car) between the two museums at a point somewhat closer to the Transport Museum. From here, you have a choice of

The Red Hand of Ulster

All over Belfast, you'll notice a curious symbol: a red hand facing you as if swearing a pledge or telling you to halt. You'll spot it, faded, above the Linen Hall Library door, in the wrought-iron fences of the Merchant Hotel, on old-fashioned clothes wringers (in the Ulster Folk Park and Transport Museum at Cultra), above the front door of a bank in Bangor, in the shape of a flowerbed at Mount Stewart House, in Loyalist paramilitary murals, on shield emblems in the gates of Republican memorials, and even on the flag of Northern Ireland (the white flag with the red cross of St. George). It's known as the Red Hand of Ulster—and it seems to pop up everywhere. It's one of the few emblems used by both communities in Northern Ireland.

Nationalists display a red-hand-on-a-yellow-shield as a symbol of the ancient province of Ulster. It was the official crest of the once-dominant O'Neill clan (who fought tooth and nail against English rule) and today signifies resistance to British rule in these communities.

But you'll more often see the red hand in Unionist areas. They see it as a potent symbol of the political entity of Northern Ireland. The Ulster Volunteer Force chose it for their symbol in 1913 and embedded it in the center of the Northern Irish flag upon partition of the island in 1921. You may see the red hand clenched as a fist in Loyalist murals. One Loyalist paramilitary group even named itself the Red Hand Commandos.

The origin of the red hand comes from a mythological tale of two rival clans that raced by boat to claim a far shore. The first clan leader to touch the shore would win it for his people. Everyone aboard both vessels strained mightily at their oars, near exhaustion as they approached the shore. Finally, in desperation, the chieftain leader of the slower boat whipped out his sword and lopped off his right hand...which he then flung onto the shore, thus winning the coveted land. Moral of the story? The fearless folk of Ulster will do *whatever it takes* to get the job done.

going downhill to the Transport Museum or uphill into the Folk Park. Assess your energy level and plan accordingly. Those with a car can drive between the museum and the folk park (otherwise, it's 200 panting yards uphill). Note that the Transport Museum is all indoors—a good bet if it's rainy. The Folk Park involves more walking between buildings spread across the upper hillside.

Visiting the Museums: The **Transport Museum** consists of three buildings. Start at the bottom and trace the evolution of transportation from 7,500 years ago—when people first decided to load an ox—to the first vertical take-off jet. In 1909, the Belfast-based Shorts Aviation Company partnered with the Wright brothers to manufacture the first commercially available aircraft. The middle building holds an intriguing section on the sinking of the Belfast-made *Titanic*. The top building covers the history of bikes, cars, and trains. The car section rumbles from the first car in Ire-

land (an 1898 Benz) through the "Cortina Culture" of the 1960s, to the local adventures of controversial automobile designer John DeLorean and a 1981 model of his sleek sports car.

The **Folk Park,** an open-air collection of 34 reconstructed buildings from all over the nine counties of Ulster, showcases the region's traditional lifestyles. After wandering through the old-town site (church, print shop, schoolhouse, humble Belfast row house, silent movie theater, and so on), you'll head off into the country to nip into cottages, farmhouses, and mills. Some houses are warmed by a wonderful peat fire and a friendly attendant. It can be dull or vibrant, depending upon when you visit and your ability to chat with the attendants. Drop a peat brick on the fire.

Carrickfergus Castle

Built during the Norman invasion of the late 1100s, this historic castle stands sentry on the shore of Belfast Lough. William of Orange landed here in 1690, when he began his Irish campaign against deposed King James II. In 1778, the American priva-teer ship *Ranger* (the first ever to fly the Stars-and-Stripes), under the com-mand of John Paul Jones, defeated the more heavily

armed HMS *Drake* just offshore. These days the castle feels a bit sanitized and geared for kids, but it's an easy excursion if you're seeking a castle experience near the city.

Cost and Hours: £5; April-Sept Mon-Sat 10:00-18:00, Sun 12:00-18:00; Oct-March Mon-Sat 10:00-16:00, Sun 14:00-16:00; last entry 30 minutes before closing, tel. 028/9335-1273.

Getting There: It's a 20-minute train ride from Belfast (on the line to Larne, £4 round-trip after 9:30, £6 before 9:30). Turn left as you exit the train station and walk straight downhill for five minutes—all the way to the waterfront—passing under the arch of the old town wall en route. You'll find the castle on your right.

Sleeping in Belfast

Belfast is more of a business town than a tourist town, so business-class room rates are lower or soft on weekends (best prices booked from their websites).

In Central Belfast

$$$ Hotel Europa is Belfast's landmark hotel—fancy, comfortable, and central—with four stars and good weekend rates. Modern yet elegant, this place was Bill Clinton's choice when he visited (Db-£90-120 plus £16 breakfast, President Clinton's suite-£400, Great Victoria Street, tel. 028/9027-1066, www.hastingshotels.com, res@eur.hastingshotels.com).

$$ Jurys Inn, an American-style hotel that rents 190 identical modern rooms, is perfectly located two blocks from City Hall (up to 3 adults or 2 adults and 2 kids for £65-110, price varies based on season and weekend rates, breakfast-£10/person, Fisherwick Place, tel. 028/9053-3500, www.jurysinns.com, jurysinnbelfast@jurysinns.com).

South of Queen's University

Many of Belfast's best budget beds cluster in a comfortable, leafy neighborhood of row houses just south of Queen's University (near the Ulster Museum). Two train stations (Botanic and Adelaide) are nearby, and buses (£1.80) zip down Malone Road every 20 minutes. Any bus on Malone Road goes to Donegall Square East. Taxis take you downtown for about £6 (your host can call one).

$$$ Malone Lodge Hotel, by far the classiest listing in this neighborhood, provides slick, business-class comfort in 92 spacious rooms on a quiet street (Sb-£79-135, Db-£95-150, superior Db-£115-155, mid-week deals, elevator, Wi-Fi, restaurant, parking, 60 Eglantine Avenue, tel. 028/9038-8000, www.malonelodgehotel-belfast.com, info@malonelodgehotel.com).

$$ Wellington Park Hotel is a dependable, if unimaginative, chain-style hotel with 75 rooms. It's predictable but in a good location (Db-£65-99, Wi-Fi, parking-£5/day, 21 Malone Road, tel. 028/9038-1111, www.wellingtonparkhotel.com, info@wellington-parkhotel.com).

$$ Camera Guest House rents 10 smoke-free rooms and has an airy, hardwood feeling throughout (S-£30-34, Sb-£40-48, Db-£55-65, family room-£70-78, 44 Wellington Park, tel. 028/9066-0026, mobile 077-4868-3174, www.cameraguesthouse.com, camera_gh@hotmail.com, Brie McCarthy).

$ Elms Village, a huge Queen's University dorm complex,

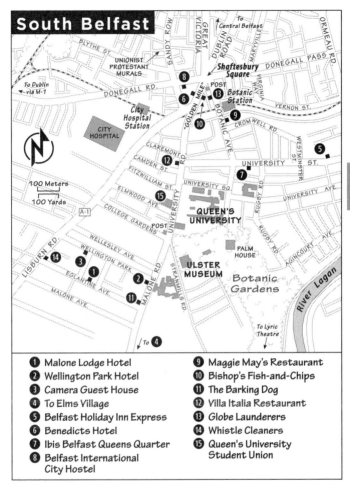

South Belfast

1. Malone Lodge Hotel
2. Wellington Park Hotel
3. Camera Guest House
4. To Elms Village
5. Belfast Holiday Inn Express
6. Benedicts Hotel
7. Ibis Belfast Queens Quarter
8. Belfast International City Hostel
9. Maggie May's Restaurant
10. Bishop's Fish-and-Chips
11. The Barking Dog
12. Villa Italia Restaurant
13. Globe Launderers
14. Whistle Cleaners
15. Queen's University Student Union

rents 100 basic, institutional rooms (mostly singles, with a few doubles) to travelers during summer break (mid-June-early-Sept only, Sb-£39, Db-£54, coin-op laundry, self-serve kitchen; reception building is 50 yards down entry street, marked *Elms Village* on low brick wall, 78 Malone Road; tel. 028/9097-4525, www.stay-atqueens.com, accommodation@qub.ac.uk).

Between Queen's University and Shaftesbury Square

$$ Belfast Holiday Inn Express is a 10-minute walk east of Queen's University. Even though it's not as central as other hotels, its 114 refurbished rooms offer a good value (Db-£69-79, better

Sleep Code

(£1 = about $1.60; country code: 44, area code: 028)
To call Belfast from the Republic of Ireland, dial 048 before the local 8-digit number.
S = Single, **D** = Double/Twin, **T** = Triple, **Q** = Quad, **b** = bathroom, **s** = shower only. Unless otherwise noted, breakfast is included and credit cards are accepted.

   To help you easily sort through these listings, I've divided the rooms into three categories, based on the price for a double room with bath:

$$$ Higher Priced—Most rooms £90 or more.
   $$ Moderately Priced—Most rooms between £60-90.
      $ Lower Priced—Most rooms £60 or less.

   Prices can change without notice; verify the hotel's current rates online or by email. For the best prices, always book direct.

deals online, kids free, elevator, by Botanic Station at 106A University Street, parking, tel. 028/9031-1909, www.exhi-belfast.com, mail@exhi-belfast.com).

$$ Benedicts Hotel has 32 rooms in a good location at the northern fringe of the Queen's University district. Its popular bar is a maze of polished wood and can be loud on weekend nights (Sb-£50-70, Db-£69-90, elevator, 7-21 Bradbury Place, tel. 028/9059-1999, www.benedictshotel.co.uk, info@benedictshotel.co.uk).

$$ Ibis Belfast Queens Quarter, part of a major European hotel chain, has 56 practical rooms in a convenient location. It's a great deal if you're not looking for cozy character (Db-£55-70, better deals online, breakfast-£7, elevator, a block north of Queen's University at 75 University Street, tel. 028/9033-3366, www.ibis-belfast.co.uk).

$ Belfast International City Hostel is big and creatively run, and provides the best value among Belfast's hostels. It has 200 beds in single and double rooms along with dorms, and is located near Botanic Station, in the heart of the lively university district. Features include free lockers, elevator, baggage storage, pay guest computer, pay Wi-Fi, kitchen, self-serve laundry (£4), a cheap breakfast-only cafeteria, 24-hour reception, and no curfew. Paul, the manager of the hostel, is a veritable TI, with a passion for his work (bed in 6-bed dorm-£11.50, bed in quad-£13, S-£22, Db-£38, 22-32 Donegall Road, tel. 028/9031-5435, www.hini.org.uk, info@hini.org.uk). The hostel is the starting point for McComb's minibus tours (described earlier, under "Tours in Belfast").

Eating in Belfast

Downtown

If it's £12 pub grub you want, consider these drinking holes with varied atmospheres.

The Morning Star is woody and elegant (£9-15 restaurant dinners upstairs, £5.50 buffet Mon-Sat 12:00-16:00; open Mon-Sat 12:00-22:00, closed Sun, down alley just off High Street at 17 Pottinger's Entry, alley entry is roughly opposite the post office, tel. 028/9023-5986).

Kelly's Cellars, once a rebel hangout (see plaque above door), still has a very gritty Irish feel. It's 300 years old and hard to find, but worth it. The pub grub is basic, but the atmosphere is delicious (Mon-Sat 11:30-24:30, Sun 13:00-23:30; live traditional music Tue-Fri and Sun at 21:30, Sat at 16:30; 32 Bank Street, 100 yards behind Tesco supermarket, access via alley on left side when facing Tesco, tel. 028/9024-6058).

Crown Liquor Saloon, a recommended stop along the Golden Mile, is small and antique. Its mesmerizing mishmash

of mosaics and shareable snugs (booths) is topped with a smoky tin ceiling (Mon-Sat lunch only 11:30-15:00, Sun 12:30-16:00, 46 Great Victoria Street, across from Hotel Europa, tel. 028/9024-3187). The **Crown Dining Room** upstairs offers dependable £10-15 meals (daily 12:00-21:00, tel. 028/9024-3187, use entry on Amelia Street when the Crown Liquor Saloon is closed).

Supermarkets: **Marks & Spencer** has a coffee shop serving skinny lattes and a supermarket in its basement (Mon-Fri 8:00-19:00, Thu until 21:00, Sat 8:00-18:00, Sun 13:00-18:00, WCs on second floor, Donegall Place, a block north of Donegall Square). **Tesco,** another supermarket, is a block north of Marks & Spencer and two blocks north of Donegall Square (Mon-Sat 8:00-19:00, Thu until 21:00, Sun 13:00-18:00, Royal Avenue and Bank Street). Picnic on the City Hall lawn.

On Waring Street, in the Cathedral Quarter

I like the cluster of culture surrounding the Cotton Court section of Waring Street. It's about a 10-minute walk northeast of the City Hall.

Check out the lobby of **Merchant Hotel** (a grand former

bank) for a glimpse of crushed-velvet Victorian splendor under an opulent dome, and consider indulging in Belfast's best afternoon tea splurge (£19.50). Don't show up in shorts and sneakers (Mon-Fri 12:00-16:30, Sat-Sun reserve ahead for two seatings: 12:30 or 15:00, 35-39 Waring Street, tel. 028/9023-4888).

Taps Wine Bar is a whiff of Mediterranean warmth in this cold brick city. Try a cheerful tapas or paella meal washed down with sangria (May-Sept daily 12:00-22:00, Oct-April closed Sun-Mon, 42 Waring Street, tel. 028/9031-1414).

The Cloth Ear is a friendly, modern bar serving better-than-average pub grub from the kitchen of the posh Merchant Hotel next door (Mon-Sat 12:30-21:00, Sun 13:00-19:00, 33 Waring Street, tel. 028/9026-2719).

Victoria Square Area

Although Victoria Square is a big, glitzy mall, a couple of eating options are worth considering—one inside the mall and one next door.

Wagamama, part of a British chain, is a Japanese noodle bar located on the first floor of the Victoria Square Mall. Hearty portions of chicken ramen, yakisoba, and cumin beef salad are menu highlights (daily 12:00-21:00, Victoria Square, tel. 028/9023-6098).

Bittles Bar is a tiny wedge-shaped throwback to Victorian days, hidden in the shadows on the east side of the mall next to the ornate, yellow Victorian fountain. The minuscule interior is decorated with caricatures of literary figures, with good pub grub served in a friendly atmosphere (daily 12:00-22:00, no food Sun, 70 Upper Church Lane just off Victoria Street, tel. 028/9031-1088).

Near Shaftesbury Square and Botanic Station

Nearby Queen's University gives this neighborhood an energetic feel, with a mixed bag of dining options ranging from cosmopolitan to deep-fried.

Maggie May's serves hearty, simple, affordable £8-12 meals (Mon-Sat 8:00-22:30, Sun 10:00-22:30, one block south of Botanic Station at 50 Botanic Avenue, tel. 028/9032-2662).

Bishop's is the locals' choice for fish-and-chips (daily 12:00-23:30, pasta and veggie options, classier side has table service and higher prices, just south of Shaftesbury Square at Bradbury Place, tel. 028/9043-9070).

South of Queen's University

The Barking Dog is closest to my cluster of accommodations in this area. It's a hip grill serving tasty burgers, duck, scallops, and other filling fare. If the weather's fine, the outdoor tree-shaded front tables are ideal for people-watching (£7-10 lunches, £12-17 dinners, Mon-Sat 12:00-15:30 & 17:30-22:00, Sun 12:00-21:00, near corner of Eglantine Avenue at 33-35 Malone Road, tel. 028/9066-1885).

Villa Italia packs in crowds hungry for linguini and *bistecca*. With its checkered tablecloths and a wood-beamed ceiling draped with grape leaves, it's a little bit of Italy in Belfast (£10-17 meals, Mon-Fri 17:00-23:00, Sat-Sun 16:00-23:00, 3 long blocks south of Shaftesbury Square, at intersection with University Street, 39 University Road, tel. 028/9032-8356).

BELFAST

Belfast Connections

For updated schedules and prices for both trains and buses in Northern Ireland, check with Translink (tel. 028/9066-6630, www.translink.co.uk). Consider a Zone 4 iLink smartcard, good for all-day train and bus use in Northern Ireland. Service is less frequent on Sundays.

If you're headed for Edinburgh or Glasgow, flying is the best use of your time. A flight takes less than an hour for not much more than the cost of the four-hour ferry plus bus or train option.

From Belfast by Train to: Dublin (8/day Mon-Sat, 5/day Sun, 2 hours), **Derry** (7/day, 2.5 hours), **Larne** (hourly, 1 hour), **Portrush** (11/day, 5/day Sun, 2 hours, transfer in Coleraine), **Bangor** (2/hour, 30 minutes).

By Bus to: Portrush (12/day, 2 hours, £8; scenic-coast route, 2.5 hours), **Derry** (hourly, 1.75 hours), **Dublin** (hourly, most via Dublin Airport, 2.75-3 hours), **Galway** (every 2 hours, 6 hours, change in Dublin), **Glasgow** (3/day, 5.75 hours), **Edinburgh** (3/day, 7 hours). The Europa Bus Centre is behind Hotel Europa (Ulsterbus tel. 028/9033-7003 for destinations in Scotland and England).

By Plane: Belfast has two airports. **George Best Belfast City Airport** (airport code: BHD, tel. 028/9093-9093, www.belfastcityairport.com) is a five-minute taxi ride from town (near the docks), while **Belfast International Airport** (airport code: BFS, tel. 028/9448-4848, www.belfastairport.com) is 18 miles west of town, connected by buses from the Europa Bus Centre behind the Europa Hotel. There are cheap flights to **Glasgow,** Scotland, on easyJet (www.easyjet.com) and Flybe (www.flybe.com).

By Ferry to Scotland: There are a couple of ports served by two companies. You can sail between Belfast and **Cairnryan** on the Stena Line ferry. A Rail Link coach connects the Cairnryan port to Ayr, where you'll catch a train to Glasgow Central station (3/day, 2.25 hours by ferry plus 2.25 hours by bus and train, £29, tel. 028/9074-7747, www.stenaline.co.uk). The less convenient P&O Ferry (toll tel. 0870-2424-777, www.poferries.com) goes from **Larne** (20 miles north of Belfast, hourly trains, 1-hour trip, TI tel. 028/2826-0088) to **Troon,** with bus or rail connections from there to Glasgow and Edinburgh.

By Ferry to England: You can sail from Belfast to **Liverpool** (generally 2/day, 8 hours, prices vary widely, arrives in port of Birkenhead—10 minutes from Liverpool, tel. 028/9074-7747, www.stenaline.co.uk).

Near Belfast

To stay in a laid-back seaside hometown—with more comfort per pound—sleep 12 miles east of Belfast in Bangor (BANG-grr). It's a handy alternative for travelers who find Belfast booked up by occasional conventions and conferences. Formerly a Victorian resort and seaside escape from the big city nearby, Bangor now has a sleepy residential feeling. To visit two worthwhile sights near Bangor—the Somme  Heritage Centre and Mount Stewart House—consider renting a car for the day from Enterprise in Bangor (10 Enterprise Road, tel. 028/9146-1616, www.enterprise.co.uk). You can also rent cars from nearby George Best Belfast City Airport, a 15-minute train trip from Bangor.

Bangor

With elegant old homes facing its spruced-up harbor and not even a hint of big-city Belfast, Bangor has appeal. The harbor is a 10-minute walk from the train station.

Getting There

Catch the train to Bangor from either Belfast's Central or Great Victoria Street stations; both are on the same line (2/hour, 30 minutes, go to the end of the line—don't get off at Bangor West). Before 9:30, it costs £8.10 round-trip (but after 9:30, it's only £5.40 round-trip). Consider stopping en route at Cultra (Ulster Folk Park and Transport Museum). The journey gives you a good, close-up look at the giant Belfast harbor cranes.

If day-tripping into Belfast from Bangor, get off at Central

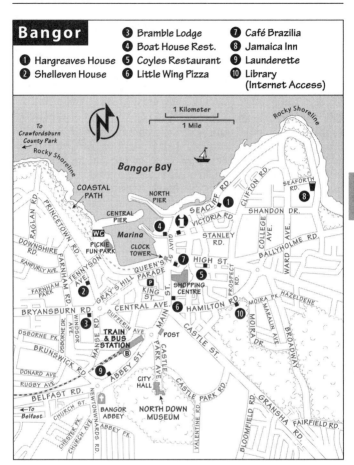

Bangor

① Hargreaves House
② Shelleven House
③ Bramble Lodge
④ Boat House Rest.
⑤ Coyles Restaurant
⑥ Little Wing Pizza
⑦ Café Brazilia
⑧ Jamaica Inn
⑨ Launderette
⑩ Library
  (Internet Access)

Station (free shuttle bus to the town center, 4/hour, none on Sun; some trains may also stop at the more convenient Great Victoria Street Station), or stay on until Botanic Station for the Ulster Museum, the Golden Mile, and Sandy Row.

Orientation to Bangor

Bangor's **TI** is in a stone tower house (from 1637) on the harborfront (Mon-Fri 9:00-17:00, Sat 10:00-17:00, Sun 13:00-17:00 except closed Sun Sept-April, 34 Quay Street, tel. 028/9127-0069, www.northdowntourism.com). You'll find **Speediwash Launderette** at 96 Abbey Street, a couple of blocks south of the train station (Mon-Fri 9:00-18:00, Sat 9:00-17:00, closed Sun, tel. 028/9127-0074). The library offers free **Internet access** (30-minute limit, Mon-Wed 9:00-21:00, Thu 9:00-22:00, Fri-Sat 9:00-17:00, closed

Sun, 80 Hamilton Road, tel. 028/9127-0591). **Bangor Cabs** provides local taxi service (tel. 028/9145-6456).

Sights in Bangor

For sightseeing, your time is better spent in Belfast. But if you have time to burn in Bangor, enjoy a walk next to the water on the **Coastal Path,** which leads west out of town from the marina. A pleasant three-mile walk along the water leads you to Crawfordsburn Country Park in the suburb of Helen's Bay. Hidden in the trees above Helen's Bay beach is Grey Point Fort, with its two WWI artillery bunkers guarding the shore (Sat-Sun 12:00-16:00, tel. 028/9185-3621). Allow 1.5 hours each way as you share the easy-to-follow and mostly paved trail with local joggers, dog walkers, and bikers.

For a shorter walk with views of the marina, head to the end of the **North Pier,** where you'll find a mosaic honoring the D-Day fleet that rendezvoused offshore in 1944, far from Nazi reconnaissance aircraft. Keep an eye out in the marina for Rose the seal. Little kids may enjoy the **Pickie Fun Park** next to the marina, with paddleboat swan rides and miniature golf.

The **North Down Museum** covers local history, from monastic days to Viking raids to Victorian splendor. It's hidden on the grassy grounds behind the City Hall, uphill and opposite from the train station (free, Tue-Sat 10:00-16:30, Sun 14:00-16:30, closed Mon, tel. 028/9127-1200).

Sleeping in Bangor

Visitors arriving in Bangor (by train) come down Main Street to reach the harbor marina. You'll find my first listing to the right, along the waterfront east of the marina on Seacliff Road. The other two listings are to the left, just uphill and west of the marina.

$$ Hargreaves House, a homey Victorian waterfront refuge with three cozy rooms, is Bangor's best value (S-£45, Sb-£50, Db-£65, large Db-£85, 10 percent discount with cash and 2-night stay—only with 2014 edition of this book in hand upon arrival, online discounts, Wi-Fi, 15-minute walk from train station but worth it, 78 Seacliff Road, tel. 028/9146-4071, mobile 079-8058-5047, www.hargreaveshouse.com, info@hargreaveshouse.com, Pauline Mendez).

$$ Shelleven House is an old-fashioned, well-kept, stately place with 11 prim rooms on the quiet corner of Princetown Road and Tennyson Avenue (Sb-£40-45, Db-£70-85, Tb-£95, 10 percent discount with cash and 2-night stay, Wi-Fi, parking, 61 Princetown Road, tel. 028/9127-1777, www.shellevenhouse.com, shellevenhouse@aol.com, Mary and Philip Weston).

$ Bramble Lodge is closest to the train station (10-minute walk), offering three inviting and spotless rooms (Sb-£40, Db-£65, Wi-Fi, 1 Bryansburn Road, tel. 028/9145-7924, jacquihanna_bramblelodge@yahoo.co.uk, Jacquiline Hanna). Ask about their simple one-bedroom self-catering apartment around the corner.

Eating in Bangor

Habitually late diners should be aware that most restaurants in town close at 21:00 and stop seating at about 20:30.

The **Boat House** is a stout stone structure hiding the finest dining experience in Bangor. It's run by two Dutch brothers who specialize in some of the freshest fish dishes in Northern Ireland. Their £20 early-bird two-course meal or £25 three-course special, offered before 19:30, are great values (Mon-Sat 12:00-21:00, Sun 12:00-20:00, reserve ahead, on Sea Cliff Road opposite the TI, tel. 028/9146-9253).

Coyles has two floors of fun. Upstairs is a classy, jazzy restaurant serving £11-17 dinners (Wed-Sun 17:00-21:00, closed Mon-Tue), while downstairs is a comfy bar with dependable pub grub (daily 12:00-15:00 & 17:00-21:00, 44 High Street, tel. 028/9127-0362).

Little Wing Pizza is a friendly joint serving tasty pizza, pasta, and salads. Grab your food to go and munch by the marina. It's also one of the few places in town that serves food later at night (daily 11:00-22:00, 37-39 Main Street, tel. 028/9147-2777).

Café Brazilia, a popular locals' hangout at lunch, is across from the stubby clock tower (Mon-Fri 8:30-20:30, Sat 8:30-16:30, closed Sun, 13 Bridge Street, tel. 028/9127-2763).

The **Jamaica Inn** offers pleasant pub grub with a breezy waterfront porch (food served from about 12:00-21:00, 10-minute walk east of the TI, 188 Seacliff Road, tel. 028/9147-1610).

Sights near Bangor

The eastern fringe of Northern Ireland is populated mostly by people who consider themselves true-blue British citizens with a history of loyalty to the Crown that goes back more than 400 years. Two sights within reach by car from Bangor highlight this area's firm roots in British culture: the Somme Heritage Centre and Mount Stewart House.

Getting There: Patchy bus service (bus #6) can be used to reach these sights from Bangor (check schedule with Bangor TI first). I'd rent a car instead. Enterprise Rent-A-Car has a handy outlet in Bangor (10 Enterprise Road, tel. 028/9146-1616, www.enterprise.co.uk). You can also rent cars from nearby George Best

Belfast City Airport, which is only 15 minutes by train from Bangor or 10 minutes from Belfast's Central Station. Because the airport is east of Belfast, your drive to these rural sights skips the headache of urban Belfast. Call ahead to confirm sight opening hours.

Somme Heritage Centre

World War I's trench warfare was a meat grinder. More British soldiers died in the last year of the war than in all of World War II. Northern Ireland's men were not spared—especially during the bloody Battle of the Somme in France, starting in July of 1916 (see the "1916" sidebar, earlier). Among the Allied forces was the British Army's 36th Ulster Division, which drew heavily from this loyal heartland of Northern Ireland. The 36th Ulster Division suffered brutal losses at the Battle of the Somme—of the 760 men recruited from the Shankill Road area in Belfast, only 10 percent survived.

Exhibits portray the battle experience through a mix of military artifacts, photos, historical newsreels, and life-size figures posed in trench warfare re-creations. To access the majority of the exhibits, it's essential to take the one-hour guided tour (leaving hourly, on the hour). Visiting this place is a moving experience, but it can only hint at the horrific conditions endured by these soldiers.

Cost and Hours: £5; July-Aug Mon-Fri 10:00-17:00, Sat-Sun 12:00-17:00; April-June and Sept Mon-Thu 10:00-16:00, Sat 12:00-16:00, closed Fri and Sun; Oct-March Mon-Thu 10:00-16:00, closed Fri-Sun; 3 miles south of Bangor just off A-21 at 233 Bangor Road, tel. 028/9182-3202, www.irishsoldier.org. A coffee shop is located at the center.

Mount Stewart House

No manor house in Ireland better illuminates the affluent lifestyle of the Protestant ascendancy than this lush estate. After the defeat of James II (the last Catholic king of England) at the Battle of

the Boyne in 1690, the Protestant monarchy was in control—and the privileged status of landowners of the same faith was assured. In the 1700s, Ireland's many Catholic rebellions seemed finally to be squashed, so Anglican landlords felt safe flaunting their wealth in manor houses surrounded by utterly perfect gardens. The Mount Stewart House in particular was designed to dazzle.

Cost and Hours: £7.40 for house and gardens, £5.60 for gardens only; July-Aug daily 12:00-18:00; May-June and Sept Wed-

Mon 13:00-18:00, closed Tue; April and Oct Thu-Sun 12:00-18:00, closed Mon-Wed; March Sat-Sun 12:00-18:00, closed weekdays; closed Nov-Feb; 8 miles south of Bangor, just off A-20 beside Strangford Lough, tel. 028/4278-8387, www.nationaltrust. org.uk.

Visiting the House: Hourly tours give you a glimpse of the cushy life led by the Marquess of Londonderry and his heirs over the past three centuries. The main entry hall is a stunner, with a black-and-white checkerboard tile floor, marble columns, classical statues, and pink walls supporting a balcony with a domed ceiling and a fine chandelier. In the dining room, you'll see the original seats occupied by the rears of European heads of state, brought back from the Congress of Vienna after Napoleon's 1815 defeat. A huge painting of Hambletonian, a prize-winning racehorse, hangs above the grand staircase, dwarfing a portrait of the Duke of Wellington in a hall nearby. The heroic duke (worried that his Irish birth would be seen as lower class by British blue bloods) once quipped in Parliament, "Just because one is born in a stable does not make him a horse." Irish emancipator Daniel O'Connell retorted, "Yes, but it could make you an ass."

Afterwards, wander the expansive manicured **gardens.** The fantasy life of parasol-toting, upper-crust Victorian society seems to ooze from every viewpoint. Fanciful sculptures of extinct dodo birds and monkeys holding vases on their heads set off predictably classic  Italian and Spanish sections. An Irish harp has been trimmed out of a hedge a few feet from a flowerbed shaped like the Red Hand of Ulster. Swans glide serenely among the lily pads on a small lake.

PORTRUSH AND THE ANTRIM COAST

The Antrim Coast—the north of Northern Ireland—is one of the most interesting and scenic coastlines in Ireland. Portrush, at the end of the train line, is an ideal base for exploring the highlights of the Antrim Coast. Within a few miles of the train terminal, you can visit evocative castle ruins, tour the world's oldest whiskey distillery, catch a thrill on a bouncy rope bridge, and hike along the famous Giant's Causeway.

Planning Your Time

You need a full day to explore the Antrim Coast, so allow two nights in Portrush. An ideal day could lace together Dunluce Castle, Old Bushmills Distillery, and the Giant's Causeway, followed by nine holes on the Portrush pitch-and-putt course. In summer months, the long days this far north extend your sightseeing time (and most golf courses stay open until dusk).

Getting Around the Antrim Coast

By Car: A car is the best way to explore the charms of the Antrim coast. Distances are short and parking is easy. If time allows, don't miss the slower-but-scenic coastal route from Portrush to Belfast via the Glens of Antrim.

By Bus: In peak season, an all-day bus pass helps you get around the region economically. The **Causeway Rambler** links Portrush to Old Bushmills Distillery, the Giant's Causeway, and the Carrick-a-Rede Rope Bridge hourly (£7/day, May-Sept only, operates roughly 10:00-17:30). The bus journey from Portrush to Carrick-a-Rede (the easternmost point of interest on the route) takes 45 minutes. Pick up a Rambler bus schedule at the TI, and buy the ticket from the driver (in Portrush, the Rambler stops at Dunluce Avenue, next to public WC, a 2-minute walk from TI; operated by Translink, tel. 028/9066-6630, www.translink.co.uk).

By Bus Tour: If you're based in Belfast, you can visit most of the sights on the Antrim Coast with a **McComb's** tour. Those based in Derry can get to the Giant's Causeway and Carrick-a-Rede Rope Bridge with **Top Tours**.

By Taxi: Groups (up to four) can reasonably visit most sights (except the more distant Carrick-a-Rede) by taxi. One-way from Portrush, it's roughly £6 to Dunluce Castle, about £8 to Old Bushmills Distillery, and about £10 to the Giant's Causeway. Try Andy Brown's Taxi (tel. 028/7082-2223), Hugh's Taxi (mobile 077-0298-6110), or North West Taxi (tel. 028/7082-4446).

Portrush

Homey Portrush used to be known as "the Brighton of the North." It first became a resort in the late 1800s, as railroads expanded to offer the new middle class a weekend by the shore. Victorian society believed that swimming in salt water would cure many common ailments.

This is County Antrim, the Bible Belt of Northern Ireland. When a large supermarket chain decided to stay open on Sundays, a local reverend called for a boycott of the store for not honoring the Sabbath. And in 2012, when the Giant's Causeway Visitors Centre opened, local Creationists demanded their viewpoint (that, according to the Bible, earth was only 6,000 years old) be represented beside modern geologic explanations of the age of the unique rock formations...carbon dating be damned.

While it's seen its best days, Portrush retains the atmosphere and architecture of a genteel seaside resort. Its peninsula is filled with lowbrow, family-oriented amusements, fun eateries, and B&Bs. Summertime fun-seekers promenade along the tiny harbor and tumble down to the sandy beaches, which extend in sweeping white crescents on either side.

Superficially, Portrush has the appearance of any small British seaside resort, but its history and large population of young people (students from nearby University of Ulster at Coleraine) give the town a little more personality. Along with the usual arcade amusements, there are nightclubs, restaurants, summer theater productions (July-Aug) in the town hall, and convivial pubs that attract customers all the way from Belfast.

Orientation to Portrush

Portrush's pleasant and easily walkable town center features sea views in every direction. On one side are the harbor and most of the restaurants, and on the other are Victorian townhouses and vast, salty vistas. The tip of the peninsula is filled with tennis courts, lawn-bowling greens, putting greens, and a park.

The town is busy with students during the school year. July and August are beach-resort boom time. June and September are laid-back and lazy. There's a brief but intense spike in visitors in late May for a huge annual motorcycle race (see "Helpful Hints," later). Families pack Portrush on Saturdays, and revelers from Belfast crowd its hotels on Saturday nights.

Tourist Information

The TI is moving in 2014, and will likely be found at the very central Town Hall—ask around (July-Aug daily 9:00-18:00; April-June and Sept Mon-Fri 9:30-17:00, Sat-Sun 12:00-17:00; March and Oct Sat-Sun 12:00-17:00, closed Mon-Fri; closed Nov-Feb; tel. 028/7082-3333). Get the Collins Northern Ireland road map (£5), the free *Visitor Attractions* brochure, and—if you're Belfast-bound—a free Belfast map.

Arrival in Portrush

The train tracks stop at the base of the tiny peninsula that Portrush fills (no baggage storage at station). All of my listed B&Bs are within a 10-minute walk of the train station. The bus stop is two blocks from the train station.

Helpful Hints

Crowds: Over a four-day weekend in late May, thousands of diehard motorcycle fans converge on Portrush, Port Stewart, and Coleraine to watch the **Northwest 200 Race.** Fearless racers scorch the roads at 200 miles per hour on the longest straightaway in motorsports. Accommodations fill up a year ahead, and traffic is the pits (dates and details at www.northwest200. org).

Phone Tips: To call the Republic of Ireland from Northern Ireland, dial 00-353, then the area code without its initial 0, and finally the local number. To call Northern Ireland from the Republic of Ireland, dial 048, and then the local eight-digit number.

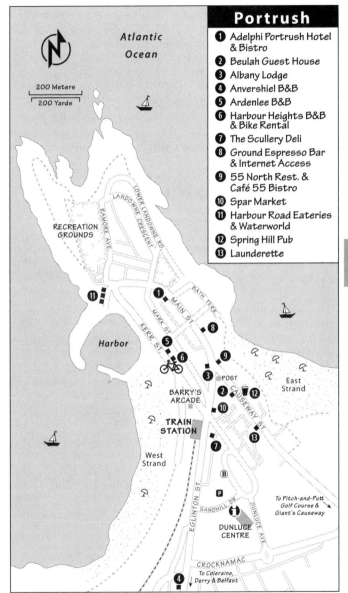

Portrush

1. Adelphi Portrush Hotel & Bistro
2. Beulah Guest House
3. Albany Lodge
4. Anvershiel B&B
5. Ardenlee B&B
6. Harbour Heights B&B & Bike Rental
7. The Scullery Deli
8. Ground Espresso Bar & Internet Access
9. 55 North Rest. & Café 55 Bistro
10. Spar Market
11. Harbour Road Eateries & Waterworld
12. Spring Hill Pub
13. Launderette

Atlantic Ocean

200 Meters
200 Yards

RECREATION GROUNDS

Harbor

LOWER LANDOWNE RD.
LANDOWNE CRESCENT
RAMORE AVE.

BATH TERR.
MAIN ST.
MARK ST.
KERR ST.

Harbor

POST

East Strand

BARRY'S ARCADE

TRAIN STATION

West Strand

CAUSEWAY ST.

To Pitch-and-Putt Golf Course & Giant's Causeway

SANDHILL DR.
EGLINTON ST.
DUNLUCE AVE.

DUNLUCE CENTRE

CROCKNAMAC
To Coleraine, Derry & Belfast

Internet Access: Ground Espresso Bar has coin-op machines with fast connections (£1/20 minutes, daily June-Aug 8:30-22:00, Sept-May 8:30-18:00, 52 Main Street, tel. 028/7082-5979).

Laundry: Viking Launderette charges £10/load for full service (Mon-Tue and Thu-Fri 9:00-13:00 & 14:00-17:30, Sat 9:00-13:00, closed Sun and Wed, 68 Causeway Street, tel. 028/7082-2060).

Bike Rental: The recommended **Harbour Heights B&B** rents sturdy new mountain bikes for £12/day, a great way to experience the gorgeous Antrim Coast (see listing under "Sleeping in Portrush," later).

PORTRUSH & ANTRIM COAST

Sights in Portrush

Barry's Old Time Amusement Arcade
This is a fine chance to see Northern Ireland at play (open weekends and summer only). Located just below the train station on the harbor, it's filled with "candy floss" (cotton candy) stands and little kids learning the art of one-armed bandits, 10p at a time. Get £1 worth of 10p coins from the machine and go wild, or brave the roller coaster and bumper cars (July-mid-Sept daily 12:30-22:30; May-June Mon-Fri 10:00-18:00, Sat 12:30-22:30, Sun 12:30-21:30; closed mid-Sept-April; tel. 028/7082-2340, www.barrysamusements.com).

Pitch-and-Putt at the Royal Portrush Golf Club
Irish courses, like those in Scotland, are highly sought after for their lush greens in glorious settings. Serious golfers can get a tee time at the Royal Portrush, which has hosted the British Open and Irish Open (green fees Mon-Fri-£145, Sat-Sun-£165). Those on a budget can play the adjacent, slightly shorter Valley Course (green fees Mon-Fri-£42.50, Sat-Sun-£55). Meanwhile, rookies can get a wee dose of this wonderful golf setting at the neighboring Skerries 9 Hole Links pitch-and-putt range. You get two clubs and balls for £8, and they don't care if you go around twice (daily 8:30-19:00, 10-minute walk from station, tel. 028/7082-2311, www.royalportrushgolfclub.com).

Portrush Recreation Grounds
For some easygoing exercise right in town, this well-organized park offers lawn-bowling greens (£4.70/hour with gear), putting greens, tennis courts, a great kids' play park, and a snack bar. You can rent tennis shoes, balls, and rackets, all for £9.30/hour (mid-May-mid-Sept Mon-Sat 10:00-dusk, Sun 13:00-19:00, closed mid-Sept-mid-May, tel. 028/7082-4441).

More Fun

Consider **Dunluce Centre** (kid-oriented fun zone) and **Waterworld** (£4.75, pool, waterslides, bowling; June Mon-Fri 10:00-15:00, Sat 10:00-17:00, Sun 12:00-17:00, July-Aug Mon-Sat 10:00-19:00, Sun 12:00-19:00; closed Sept-May; wedged between Harbour Bistro and Ramore Wine Bar, tel. 028/7082-2001).

Sleeping in Portrush

Portrush has a range of hotels, from decent to ritzy. Some B&Bs can be well-worn. August and Saturday nights can be tight (and loud) with young party groups. Otherwise, it's a "you take half a loaf when you can get it" town. Rates vary with the view and season—probe for softness. Many listings face the sea, though sea views are worth paying for only if you get a bay window. Ask for a big room (some doubles can be very small; twins are bigger). Lounges are invariably grand and have bay-window views. All places listed have lots of stairs, but most are perfectly central and within a few minutes' walk of the train station. Parking is easy.

$$ Adelphi Portrush is a breath of fresh air, with 28 tastefully furnished modern rooms, friendly staff, and a hearty bistro downstairs (Sb-£55-105, Db-£65-115, Tb-£75-135, Qb-£105-165, 67-71 Main Street, Wi-Fi, tel. 028/7082-5544, www.adelphiportrush.com, stay@adelphiportrush.com).

$ Beulah Guest House is a traditional, good-value place. It's centrally located and run by cheerful Rachel and Jimmy Anderson, with 11 prim and smoke-free rooms (Ss-£33, Sb-£45-60, Db-£60-75, Tb-£85-95, Wi-Fi, parking at rear, 16 Causeway Street, tel. 028/7082-2413, www.beulahguesthouse.com, stay@beulahguesthouse.com).

$ Albany Lodge is a rejuvenated 85-year-old guesthouse smack dab in the center of town. Kate and Gwynne Fletcher create an upbeat vibe with their nine bright rooms, many with scenic sea views (Sb-£45-79, Db-£50-95, Tb-£75-85, ask about 2-night deals, Wi-Fi, 2 Eglinton Street, tel. 028/7082-3492, www.albanylodge.net, albanylodge@hotmail.co.uk).

$ Anvershiel B&B, with six rooms, is a 10-minute walk south of the train station. Jovial Victor Bow, who runs the show with his wife Erna, knows about local golf options (Sb-£45, Db-£65, Tb-£95, Qb-£125, cash only, Wi-Fi, parking, 16 Coleraine Road, tel. 028/7082-3861, www.anvershiel.com, enquiries@anvershiel.com).

$ Ardenlee B&B offers six good rooms, some with fine views of the ocean (Sb-£35-50, Db-£60-90, Tb-£100, Wi-Fi, 19 Kerr Street, tel. 028/7082-2639, mobile 078-0725-9460, www.ardenleehouse.com, russell.rafferty@btconnect.com).

Sleep Code

(£1 = about $1.60, country code: 44, area code: 028)
To call Portrush from the Republic of Ireland, dial 048 before the local 8-digit number.

S = Single, **D** = Double/Twin, **T** = Triple, **Q** = Quad, **b** = bathroom, **s** = shower only. Breakfast is included and credit cards are accepted unless otherwise noted.

To help you easily sort through these listings, I've divided the accommodations into two categories, based on the price for a standard double room with bath:

$$ **Higher Priced**—Most rooms £80 or more.

$ **Lower Priced**—Most rooms less than £80.

Prices can change without notice; verify the hotel's current rates online or by email. For the best prices, always book direct.

$ Harbour Heights B&B rents nine homey rooms, each named after a different town in County Antrim. It has an inviting guest lounge overlooking the harbor, and friendly South African hosts Sam and Tim Swart (Sb-£40, Db-£70-80, family rooms, Wi-Fi, bike rentals, 17 Kerr Street, tel. 028/7082-2765, mobile 078-9586-6534, www.harbourheightsportrush.com, info@harbourheightsportrush.com).

Eating in Portrush

Being both a get-away-from-Belfast and close-to-a-university town (Coleraine), Portrush has more than enough chips joints. Eglinton Street is lined with cheap and cheery eateries.

Lunch Spots

The Scullery is a tiny hole-in-the-wall, making sandwiches and healthy wraps to take away and enjoy by the beach—or on an Antrim Coast picnic (Mon-Sat 9:00-17:00, Sun 10:00-16:00, close to the train station at 4 Eglinton Lane, tel. 028/7082-1000).

Ground Espresso Bar makes fresh £4 sandwiches or paninis, soup, and excellent coffee (daily June-Aug 9:00-22:00, Sept-May 9:00-17:00, 52 Main Street, tel. 028/7082-5979). They also offer coin-op Internet access (see "Helpful Hints," earlier).

Café 55 Bistro serves basic sandwiches with a great patio view (May-Sept Mon-Fri 9:00-17:00, Sat-Sun 9:00-21:30, shorter hours off-season, 1 Causeway Street, beneath fancier 55 North restaurant run by same owners—listed below, tel. 028/7082-2811).

The **Spar Market** has what you'll need for your Antrim Coast picnic (Mon-Sat 7:00-20:00, Sun 7:00-19:00, across from Barry's Arcade on Main Street, tel. 028/7082-5447).

Fine Dining

55 North (named for the local latitude) has the best sea views in town, with windows on three sides. The classy pasta-and-fish plates are a joy (£10-17 plates, daily 12:30-14:00 & 17:00-21:00 except closed Mon Sept-June, 1 Causeway Street, tel. 028/7082-2811).

Adelphi Bistro is a good bet for its relaxed, family-friendly atmosphere and hearty meals (daily 12:00-15:00 & 17:00-21:00, 67-71 Main Street, tel. 028/7082-5544).

Harbour Road Eateries

The following restaurants, located within 50 yards of each other (all under the same ownership and overlooking the harbor on Harbour Road), offer some of the best food values in town.

Ramore Wine Bar—salty, modern, and much-loved—bursts with happy eaters. They have the most inviting menu that I've seen in Ireland, featuring huge meals ranging from steaks to vegetarian food. Share a piece of the decadent banoffee (banana toffee) pie with a friend (£9-15 plates, daily 12:15-14:15 & 17:00-21:30, Sun until 21:00, tel. 028/7082-4313).

Downstairs, sharing the same building as the Ramore Wine Bar, is the energetic **Coast Pizzeria,** with great Italian dishes. Come early for a table, or sit at the bar (Mon-Fri 17:00-21:30, Sat 16:30-22:00, Sun 15:00-21:00; Sept-June closed Mon-Tue; tel. 028/7082-3311).

The **Harbour Bistro** offers a more subdued, darker bistro ambience than the previous two eateries, with meals for a few pounds more (£9-16 dinners, daily 17:00-21:30, tel. 028/7082-2430).

Pubs

The **Harbour Bar** (next to the Harbour Bistro) has an old-fashioned pub downstairs and a plush, overstuffed, dark lounge upstairs. Or try the **Spring Hill Pub** (17 Causeway Street, tel. 028/7082-3361), with a friendly vibe and occasional music session nights.

Portrush Connections

Consider a £16.50 Zone 4 iLink smartcard, good for all-day train and bus use in Northern Ireland year-round (£15 top-up for each additional day). Translink has useful updated schedules and prices for both trains and buses in Northern Ireland (tel. 028/9066-6630, www.translink.co.uk).

From Portrush by Train to: Coleraine (hourly, 12 minutes,

PORTRUSH & ANTRIM COAST

sparse on Sun morning), **Belfast** (11/day, 5/day Sun, 2 hours, transfer in Coleraine), **Dublin** (7/day, 2/day Sun, 5 hours, transfer in Coleraine or Belfast).

By Bus to: Belfast (12/day, 2 hours; scenic coastal route, 2.5 hours), **Dublin** (4/day, 5.5 hours).

Antrim Coast

The craggy 20-mile stretch of the Antrim Coast extending eastward from Portrush to Ballycastle rates second only to the tip of the Dingle Peninsula as the prettiest chunk of coastal Ireland. From your base in Portrush, you have a varied grab bag of sightseeing choices: the Giant's Causeway, Old Bushmills Distillery, Dunluce Castle, Carrick-a-Rede Rope Bridge, and Rathlin Island.

It's easy to weave these sights together by car, but connections are patchy by public transportation. Bus service is viable only in summer, and taxi fares are reasonable only for the sights closest to Portrush (Dunluce Castle and the Old Bushmills Distillery). For more on your transportation options, see "Getting Around the Antrim Coast," earlier.

Planning Your Time

With a car, you can visit the Giant's Causeway, Old Bushmills Distillery, Carrick-a-Rede Rope Bridge, and Dunluce Castle in one busy day. Call ahead to reserve the Old Bushmills Distillery tour, and get an early start. Arrive at the Giant's Causeway by 9:00, when crowds are sparse. Park your car in the visitors center lot (opens at 9:00; parking is included with your entry fee). Early birds will find that the trails are free and always open. Spend an hour and a half scrambling over Ireland's most unique geology.

Then catch a late-morning tour of the Old Bushmills Distillery. Grab a cheap lunch in the hospitality room afterwards. A 20-minute drive east brings you to Carrick-a-Rede, where you can enjoy a scenic cliff-top trail hike all the way to the lofty rope bridge (one hour round-trip, 1.5 hours if you cross the rope bridge and explore the sea stack). Hop in your car and double back west all the way to dramatically cliff-perched Dunluce Castle for a late-afternoon tour. From here, you're only a five-minute drive from Portrush.

Those with extra time, a car, and a hankering to seek out dramatic coastal cliff scenery may want to spend a half-day boating out to Rathlin Island, Northern Ireland's only inhabited island.

The Scottish Connection

The Romans called the Irish the "Scoti" (meaning pirates). When the Scoti crossed the narrow Irish Sea and invaded the

land of the Picts 1,500 years ago, that region became known as Sco-ti-land. Ireland and Scotland were never conquered by the Romans, and they retained similar clannish Celtic traits. Both share the same Gaelic branch of the linguistic tree.

On clear summer days from Carrick-a-Rede, the island of Mull in Scotland—only 17 miles away—is visible. Much closer on the horizon is the boomerang-shaped Rathlin Island, part of Northern Ireland. Rathlin is where Scottish leader Robert the Bruce (a compatriot of William "Braveheart" Wallace) retreated in 1307 after defeat at the hands of the English. Legend has it that he hid in a cave on the island, where he observed a spider patiently rebuilding its web each time a breeze knocked it down. Inspired by the spider's perseverance, Robert gathered his Scottish forces once more and finally defeated the English at the decisive battle of Bannockburn.

Flush with confidence from his victory, Robert the Bruce decided to open a second front against the English...in Ireland. In 1315, he sent his brother Edward over to enlist their Celtic Irish cousins in an effort to thwart the English. After securing Ireland, Edward hoped to move on and enlist the Welsh, thus cornering England with their pan-Celtic nation. But Edward's timing was bad—Ireland was in the midst of famine. His Scottish troops had to live off the land and began to take food and supplies from the starving Irish. He might also have been trying to destroy Ireland's crops to keep them from being used as a colonial "breadbasket" to feed English troops. The Scots quickly wore out their welcome, and Edward the Bruce was eventually killed in battle near Dundalk in 1318.

This was the first time in history that Ireland was used as a pawn by England's enemies. Spain and France saw Ireland as the English Achilles' heel, and both countries later attempted invasions of the island. The English Tudor and Stuart royalty countered these threats in the 16th and 17th centuries by starting the "plantation" of loyal subjects in Ireland. The only successful long-term settlement by the English was here in Northern Ireland, which remains part of the United Kingdom today.

It's interesting to imagine how things might be different today if Ireland and Scotland had been permanently welded together as a nation 700 years ago. You'll notice the strong Scottish influence in this part of Ireland when you ask a local a question and he answers, "Aye, a wee bit." The Irish joke that the Scots are just Irish people who couldn't swim home.

Sights on the Antrim Coast

▲▲Giant's Causeway

This five-mile-long stretch of coastline, a World Heritage Site, is famous for its bizarre basalt columns. The shore is covered with

largely hexagonal pillars that stick up at various heights. It's as if the earth were offering God his choice of 37,000 six-sided cigarettes.

Geologists claim the Giant's Causeway was formed by volcanic eruptions more than 60 million years ago. As the surface of the lava flow quickly cooled, it contracted and crystallized into columns (resembling the caked mud at the bottom of a dried-up lakebed, but with deeper cracks). As the rock later settled and eroded, the columns broke off into the many stair-like steps that now honeycomb the Antrim Coast.

Of course, in actuality, the Giant's Causeway was made by a giant Ulster warrior named Finn MacCool who knew of a rival giant living on the Scottish island of Staffa. Finn built a stone bridge over to Staffa to spy on his rival, and found out that the Scottish giant was much bigger. Finn retreated back to Ireland and had his wife dress him as a sleeping infant, just in time for the rival giant to come across the causeway to spy on Finn. The rival, shocked at the infant's size, fled back to Scotland in terror of whomever had sired this giant baby. Breathing a sigh of relief, Finn tore off the baby clothes and prudently knocked down the bridge. Today, proof of this encounter exists in the geologic formation that still extends undersea and surfaces at Staffa.

Giant's Causeway Visitors Centre

For cute variations on the Finn story, as well as details on the ridiculous theories of modern geologists, start out in the visitors center. It's filled with interactive exhibits giving a worthwhile history of the Giant's Causeway, with a regional overview. On the far wall opposite the entrance, check out the interesting three-minute film showing the evolution of the causeway from molten lava to the geometric, geologic wonderland of today. The large 3-D model of the causeway offers a bird's-eye view of the region. Some of the exhibits are geared to kids who get a kick out of all things giant-related. A gift shop and cafe are standing by.

Cost and Hours: £8.50 (includes parking), open daily 9:00-18:00; hiking trails free and open from dawn to dusk; tel. 028/2073-1855, www.nationaltrust.org.uk/giantscauseway.

Visiting the Causeway

The causeway itself—the highlight of the entire coast—is free and always open. If you pay to enter the visitor's center, you can borrow a great little **audioguide** to take along on your hike. Each of the audioguide's 15 stops displays a photo of the formation being described to help you better recognize each one as you walk; all stops are shown on the map you'll receive with your ticket.

From the visitors center, you have several options for visiting the causeway:

By Minibus: A minibus (4/hour from 9:00, £1 each way) zips tired tourists a half-mile directly from the visitors center down a paved road and along the tidal zone to the causeway. This standard route (the blue dashed line on your map) offers the easiest access and follows the stops on your audioguide. Some choose to walk down this route to the causeway, and then take the shuttle back up.

By Foot: For a better dose of the causeway, consider the cliff-top trail (red dashed line on your map). Take the easy-to-follow trail uphill from the visitors center 10 minutes and catch your breath at Weir's Snout, the great fence-protected precipice viewpoint. It's only 15 level minutes farther to reach the Shepherd's Steps. Then grab the banister on the steep stairs and zigzag down the switchbacks towards the water; at the T-junction, go 100 yards right, to the towering rock pipes of "the Organ." (You can walk another 500 yards east around the headland, but the trail dead-ends there.) Now retrace your steps west on the trail (don't go up the steps again), continuing down to the tidal zone, where the "Giant's Boot" (six feet tall, on the right) provides some photo fun. Another 100 yards farther is the dramatic point where the causeway meets the sea. Just beyond that, at the asphalt turnaround, is the bus stop where you can catch a shuttle bus back to the visitors center. Or walk back up, listening to the audioguide at the highlighted stops.

The Full Monty: Hardy hikers can spend a couple of hours exploring the trail that runs along a five-mile section of the Causeway Coast (yellow dashed line on your map). However, occasional rock falls and slides can close this route (ask first at Portrush TI, or call ahead to visitors center). A £1 hiking guide, sold at the TI, points out the highlights named by 18th-century guides (Camel's Back, Giant's Eye, and so on).

A good plan is to take the Causeway Rambler bus or a taxi from Portrush to the meager ruins of Dunseverick Castle (east of Giant's Causeway on B-146). Get off there and hike west, following the cliff-hugging contours of Benbane Head back to the visitors center. Then travel back to Portrush by taxi or Rambler bus (check bus schedules ahead of time at Portrush TI or online at www.translink.co.uk).

PORTRUSH & ANTRIM COAST

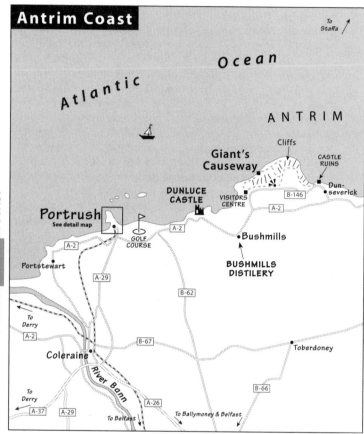

▲▲Old Bushmills Distillery

Bushmills claims to be the world's oldest distillery. Though King James I (of Bible fame) only granted Bushmills its license to distill "Aqua Vitae" in 1608, whiskey has been made here since the 13th century. Distillery tours waft you through the process, making it clear that Irish whiskey is triple distilled—and therefore smoother than Scotch whisky (distilled merely twice and minus the "e"). The 45-minute tour starts with the mash pit, which is filled with a porridge that eventually becomes whiskey. (The leftovers of that porridge are fed to the county's particularly happy cows.) You'll see thousands of oak casks—the kind used for Spanish sherry—filled with aging whiskey.

The finale, of course, is the opportunity for a sip in the 1608 Bar—the former malt barn. Visitors get a single glass of their choice. Hot-drink enthusiasts might enjoy a cinnamon-and-cloves hot toddy. Teetotalers can just order tea, totally.

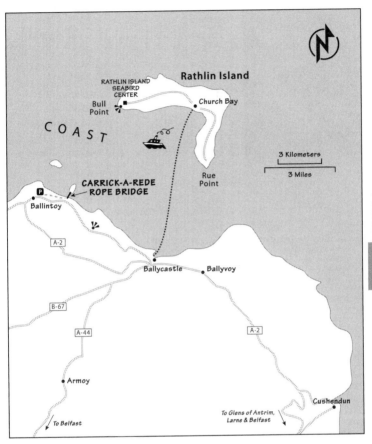

To see the distillery at its lively best, visit when the 100 workers are staffing the machinery—Monday morning through Friday noon (weekend tours see a still still). Tours are limited to 35 people and book up. In summer, call ahead to put in your name and get a tour time. After the tour, you can get a decent lunch in the tasting room.

Cost and Hours: £7; April-Oct tours on the half-hour Mon-Sat from 9:30, Sun from 12:00, last tour at 16:00; Nov-March tours Mon-Sat at 10:00, 11:00, 12:00, 13:30, 14:30, and 15:30, Sun from 12:00. To find Bushmills, look for the distillery sign a quarter-mile from Bushmills town center. Tel. 028/2073-3218, www.bushmills.com.

▲▲Carrick-a-Rede Rope Bridge

For 200 years, fishermen have hung a narrow, 90-foot-high bridge (planks strung between wires) across a 65-foot-wide chasm be-

tween the mainland and a tiny island. Today, the bridge (while not the original version) still gives access to the salmon nets that are set during summer months to catch the fish turning the coast's corner. (The complicated system is described at the gateway.) A pleasant, 30-minute, one-mile walk from the parking lot takes you to the rope bridge. Cross over to the island for fine views and great seabird-watching, especially during nesting season.

Cost and Hours: £5.60 trail and bridge fee, pay at hut beside parking lot, coffee shop and WCs near parking lot; March-Oct daily 9:30-18:00, June-Aug until 19:00; Nov-Feb 10:00-14:30; tel. 028/2076-9839, www.nationaltrust.org.uk.

Nearby: If you have a car and a picnic lunch, don't miss the terrific coastal **viewpoint** rest area one mile steeply uphill and east of Carrick-a-Rede (on B-15 to Ballycastle). This grassy area offers one of the best picnic views in Northern Ireland (picnic tables but no WCs). Feast on bird's-eye views of the rope bridge, nearby Rathlin Island, and the not-so-distant Island of Mull in Scotland.

▲Dunluce Castle

These romantic ruins, perched dramatically on the edge of a rocky headland, are a testimony to this region's turbulent past. During the Middle Ages, the castle re-sisted several sieges. But on a stormy night in 1639, dinner was interrupted as half of the kitchen fell into the sea and took the servants with it (Ireland's first fast food?). That was the last straw for the lady of the castle. The countess of Antrim packed up and moved inland, and the  castle "began its slow submission to the forces of nature." While it's one of the largest castles in Northern Ireland and is beautifully situated, there's precious little left to see among its broken walls.

The 16th-century expansion of the castle was financed by the salvaging of a shipwreck. In 1588, the Spanish Armada's *Girona*—overloaded with sailors and the valuables of three abandoned sister ships—sank on her way home after the aborted mission against England. More than 1,300 drowned, and only five survivors washed ashore. The shipwreck was excavated in 1967, and a bounty of golden odds and silver ends wound up in Belfast's Ulster Museum.

Castle admission includes an impromptu guided tour of the ruins given by a small stable of dedicated guides. Before entering, catch the great seven-minute film about the history of the castle (across from the ticket desk).

Cost and Hours: £5, free audioguide, daily April-Sept 10:00-17:30, Oct-March 10:00-16:00, last entry 30 minutes before closing, tel. 028/2073-1938.

Rathlin Island

The only inhabited island off the coast of Northern Ireland, Rathlin is a quiet haven for hikers, birdwatchers, and seal spotters. Less

than seven miles from end to end, this "L"-shaped island is reachable by ferry from the town of Ballycastle.

Getting There: The Rathlin Island ferry departs from Ballycastle, just east of Carrick-a-Rede. It does 10 crossings per day in summer. Six are fast 20-minute trips on passenger boats, and four are slower 45-minute trips on car ferries (£12 round-trip per passenger on either type of boat, reserve ahead, tel. 028/2076-9299, www.rathlinballycastleferry.com).

Travelers with rental cars will have no problem reaching Ballycastle. A taxi from Portrush to Ballycastle runs £25 one-way. Bus service from Portrush to Ballycastle is spotty (check with the TI in Portrush, or contact Translink—tel. 028/9066-6630, www.translink.co.uk).

Visiting Rathlin Island: Rathlin's population of 75 islanders clusters around the ferry dock at Church Bay. Here you'll find the Rathlin Manor House, offering the island's most convenient lodging, a restaurant, and a pub (tel. 028/2076-3964, www.rathlinmanorhouse.co.uk). The **Rathlin Boathouse Visitor Centre** operates as the island's TI (May-Aug daily 10:30-13:30 & 14:00-16:00, on the bay 100 yards east of the ferry dock, tel. 028/2076-2225).

In summer, the Puffin shuttle bus (£5 round-trip, seats 25) meets arriving ferries and drives visitors to the **Rathlin Island Seabird Centre** at the west end of the island. Here a lighthouse extends down the cliff with its beacon at the bottom. It's upside down because the coast guard wants the light visible only from a certain distance out to sea. The bird observation terrace at the center (next to the lighthouse) overlooks one of the most dramatic coastal views in Ireland—a sheer drop of more than 300 feet to craggy sea stacks just offshore that are draped in thousands of sea birds. Photographers will want to bring their most powerful zoom lens.

For such a snoozy island, Rathlin has seen its fair share of history. Flint axe-heads were quarried here in Neolithic times. The island was one of the first in Ireland to be raided by Vikings, in 795. Robert the Bruce hid out from English pursuers on Rathlin in the early 1300s (see "The Scottish Connection" sidebar, earlier). In the late 1500s, local warlord Sorely Boy MacDonnell stashed his extended family on Rathlin and waited on the mainland at Dunluce Castle to face his English enemies...only to watch in horror as they headed for the island instead to massacre his loved ones. And in 1917, a WWI U-boat sank the British cruiser HMS *Drake* in Church Bay. The wreck is now a popular scuba-dive destination.

▲Antrim Mountains and Glens

Not particularly high (never more than 1,500 feet), the Antrim Mountains are cut by a series of large glens running northeast to the sea. Glenariff, with its waterfalls (especially the Mare's Tail), is the most beautiful of the nine glens. Travelers going by car can take a pleasant drive from Portrush to Belfast, sticking to the A-2 road that takes in parts of all of the Glens of Antrim. The two best stops en route are Cushendall (nice beach for a picnic) and the castle at Carrickfergus.

DERRY AND COUNTY DONEGAL

The town of Derry (or Londonderry to Unionists) is the mecca of Ulster Unionism. When Ireland was being divvied up, the River Foyle was the logical border between the North and the Republic. But, for sentimental and economic reasons, the North kept Derry, which is on the Republic's side of the river. Consequently, this predominantly Catholic city has been much contested throughout the Troubles.

Even its name is disputed. While most of its population and its city council call it "Derry," some maps, road signs, and all train schedules in the UK use "Londonderry," the name on its 1662 royal charter and the one favored by Unionists. I once asked a Northern Ireland rail employee for a ticket to "Derry"; he replied that there was no such place, but he would sell me one to "Londonderry."

Still, the conflict is only one dimension of Derry; this pivotal city has a more diverse history and a prettier setting than Belfast. Derry was a vibrant city back when Belfast was just a mudflat. With a quarter of Belfast's population (85,000), Derry feels more welcoming and manageable to visitors.

County Donegal, to the west of Derry, is about as far-flung as Ireland gets. A forgotten economic backwater (part of the Republic but riding piggyback on the North), it lacks blockbuster museums or sights. But a visit here is more about the journey, and adventurous drivers—a car is a must—will be rewarded with a time-capsule peek into old Irish ways and starkly beautiful scenery.

Planning Your Time

Travelers heading north from Westport or Galway should get an early start. Donegal town makes a good lunch stop, with lots of choices surrounding its triangular town square. And then it's on to Derry, where you can spend a couple of hours seeing the essentials: Visit the Tower Museum and catch some views from the town wall before continuing on to Portrush for the night.

With more time, spend a night in Derry, so you can see the powerful Bogside murals (illuminated after dark) and take a walking tour around the town walls—you'll appreciate this underrated city. With two nights in Derry, consider crossing the border into the Republic for a scenic driving loop through part of remote County Donegal.

Derry

No city in Ireland connects the kaleidoscope of historical dots more colorfully than Derry. From a leafy monastic hamlet to a Viking-pillaged port, from a cannonball-battered siege survivor to an Industrial Revolution sweatshop, from an essential WWII naval base to a wrenching flashpoint of sectarian Troubles...Derry has seen it all.

But the past few years have brought some refreshing changes. Manned British Army surveillance towers were taken down in 2006, and most British troops finally departed in mid-2007, after 38 years in Northern Ireland. In June of 2011, a new, curvy pedestrian bridge across the River Foyle was completed. Locals have dubbed it the "Peace Bridge" because it links the predominantly Protestant Waterside (east bank) with the predominantly Catholic Cityside (west bank). Today, you can feel comfortable wandering the streets and enjoying this "legend-Derry" Irish city.

Orientation to Derry

The River Foyle flows north, slicing Derry into eastern and western chunks. The old town walls and almost all worthwhile sights are on the west side. (The train station and Ebrington Square—at the end of the Peace Bridge—are the main reasons to set foot on the east side.) Waterloo Place and the adjacent Guildhall Square, just outside the north corner of the old city walls, are the pedestrian hubs of city activity. The Strand Road area extending north from Waterloo Place makes a comfortable home base, with the majority of lodging and restaurant suggestions within a block or two on either side. The Diamond and its War Memorial statue mark the heart of the old city within the walls.

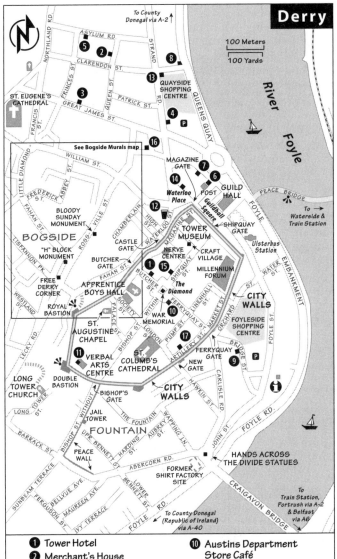

Derry

To County Donegal via A-2 ↑

N

100 Meters
100 Yards

NORTHLAND RD.

ASYLUM RD.

❺ ❷

CLARENDON ST.

STRAND RD.

❽

PRINCES ST.

QUEEN ST.

❸

GREAT JAMES ST.

PATRICK ST.

QUEENS QUAY

❹ P

❻

QUAYSIDE SHOPPING CENTRE

ST. EUGENE'S CATHEDRAL

FRANCIS ST.

River Foyle

❶❻

See Bogside Murals map

WILLIAM ST.

LITTLE DIAMOND

FREDERICK ST.

ABBEY ST.

FAHAN ST.

ROSSVILLE ST.

BLOODY SUNDAY MONUMENT

MAGAZINE GATE

❼

❶❹

Waterloo Place

❻

POST

GUILD HALL

PEACE BRIDGE

To → Waterside & Train Station

BOGSIDE

"H" BLOCK MONUMENT

CHAMBERLAIN ST.

CASTLE GATE

❶❷

HIGH ST.

WATERLOO ST.

MAGAZINE ST.

Guildhall Square

SHIPQUAY GATE

TOWER MUSEUM

FOYLE ST.

UISNANNOR PK.

FREE DERRY CORNER

BUTCHER GATE

FAHAN ST.

BUTCHER ST.

NERVE CENTRE

❶ ❶❺

SHIPQUAY ST.

CRAFT VILLAGE

Ulsterbus Station

WESTLAND ST.

APPRENTICE BOYS HALL

ROYAL BASTION

SOCIETY ST.

MILLENNIUM FORUM

WATER ST.

The Diamond

❶❶

ST. AUGUSTINE'S CHAPEL

PALACE ST.

WAR MEMORIAL

WITHIN ST.

LINENHALL ST.

FERRYQUAY ST.

ORCHARD ST.

MARKET ST.

CITY WALLS

FOYLESIDE SHOPPING CENTRE

P

LECKY RD.

❶❶

VERBAL ARTS CENTRE

DOUBLE BASTION

BISHOP ST. WITHIN

LONDON ST.

ST. COLUMB'S CATHEDRAL

PUMP ST.

❶❼

ARTILLERY ST.

NEW GATE

FERRYQUAY GATE

❾

BRIDGE ST.

FOYLE ST.

ℹ

LONG TOWER CHURCH

LONG TOWER ST.

BISHOP'S GATE

CITY WALLS

HAWKIN ST.

CARLISLE RD.

JAIL TOWER

THE FOUNTAIN

WAPPING LN.

BARRACK ST.

BISHOP ST. WITHOUT

UPR. BENNETT ST.

HARDING ST.

AUBREY ST.

FOUNTAIN

PEACE WALL

ABERCORN RD.

JOHN ST.

FOYLE RD.

HANDS ACROSS THE DIVIDE STATUES

SUNBEAM TERRACE

BELLVUE AVE.

FERGUSON ST.

MAUREEN AVE.

LOWER BENNETT ST.

IVY TERRACE

FOYLE RD.

FORMER SHIRT FACTORY SITE

CRAIGAVON BRIDGE

To Train Station, Portrush via A-2 & Belfast via A6

To County Donegal (Republic of Ireland) via A-40

❶ Tower Hotel
❷ Merchant's House
❸ Saddler's House
❹ Travelodge
❺ Paddy's Palace Hostel
❻ Custom House Restaurant & Wine Bar
❼ Exchange Rest. & Wine Bar
❽ Mandarin Palace Rest.
❾ Fitzroy's Restaurant
❿ Austins Department Store Café
⓫ Bloom's Café
⓬ Peadar O'Donnell's Pub
⓭ Tesco Supermarket
⓮ SuperValu Supermarket
⓯ Internet Café
⓰ Laundry
⓱ Playhouse Theatre

DERRY & COUNTY DONEGAL

Tourist Information

The TI sits on the riverfront and offers a room-finding service, rents bikes, books bus and walking tours (see "Tours in Derry," later), and gives out free city maps (July-Sept Mon-Fri 9:00-19:00, Sat 10:00-18:00, Sun 10:00-16:00; Oct-June Mon-Fri 9:00-18:00, Sat 10:00-17:00, closed Sun; 44 Foyle Street, tel. 028/7126-7284, www.derryvisitor.com).

Arrival in Derry

Next to the river on the east side of town, Derry's little end-of-the-line train station (no storage lockers) has service to Portrush, Belfast, and Dublin. Free shuttle buses to Ulsterbus station (on the west side of town, a couple of minutes' walk south of Guildhall Square on Foyle Street) await each arriving train. Otherwise, it's a £5 taxi ride to Guildhall Square. The same free shuttle service leaves Ulsterbus station 15 minutes before each departing train. Unfortunately, there's not yet a footpath from the train station to the pedestrian Peace Bridge.

Derry is compact enough to see on foot; drivers stopping for a few hours can park at the Foyleside parking garage across from the TI (£1/hour, £3/4 hours, Mon-Tue 8:00-19:00, Wed-Fri 8:00-22:00, Sat 8:00-20:00, Sun 12:00-19:00, tel. 028/7137-7575). Drivers staying overnight can ask about parking at their B&B, or try the Quayside parking garage behind the Travelodge (£0.80/hour, £3/4 hours, £8 additional for overnight, Mon-Fri 7:30-21:00, Sat 7:30-20:00, Sun 8:30-18:00).

Helpful Hints

Phone Tips: To call the Republic of Ireland from Northern Ireland, dial 00-353, then the area code without its initial 0, and finally the local number. To call Northern Ireland from the Republic of Ireland, dial 048, and then the local eight-digit number.

Money: Danske Bank is on Guildhall Square, and the **Bank of Ireland** is on Strand Road (both open Mon-Fri 9:30-16:30, Sat 9:30-12:30, closed Sun).

Internet Access: Located inside the walls, **Claudes Café** is just north of the Diamond on Shipquay Street (£3/30 minutes, daily 9:00-17:30, tel. 028/7127-9379).

Bookstore: Foyle Books is a dusty little pleasure for random browsing (Mon-Sat 11:00-17:00, closed Sun, 12 Magazine Street at entrance to Craft Village, tel. 028/7137-2530).

Post Office: The main post office is just off Waterloo Place (Mon-Fri 9:00-17:30, Sat 9:00-12:30, closed Sun, Custom House Street).

Laundry: Smooth Operators can do a load of laundry for about

£9 (drop off in morning to pick up later that day, Mon-Fri 8:30-18:00, Sat 8:30-17:30, closed Sun, 8 Sackville Street, tel. 028/7136-0529).

Taxi: Try **The Taxi Company** (tel. 028/7126-2626) or **Foyle Taxis** (tel. 028/7126-3905).

Car Rental: Enterprise is a handy place to rent a car (tel. 028/7186-1699, 70 Clooney Road, www.enterprise.co.uk).

Tours in Derry

Walking Tours

Martin McCrossan and his staff lead insightful hour-long tours of the city, departing from 11 Carlisle Road just below Ferryquay Gate (£4; daily at 10:00, 12:00, and 14:00; call to confirm schedule; they also offer private tours—one-hour city tour-£25, four-hour Giant's Causeway or County Donegal tour-£100; tel. 028/7127-1996, mobile 077-1293-7997, www.irishtourguides.com).

Stephen McPhilemy leads private tours of Derry (his hometown), Belfast, and the North Coast—when he's not on the road guiding Rick Steves tours several months a year (tel. 028/7130-9051, mobile 078-0101-1027, www.irishexperience.ie, steve@irishexperience.ie). Stephen also runs the recommended Paddy's Palace Hostel.

Bus Tours

Top Tours' double-decker buses are a good option for a general overview of Derry. You'll be driven around the city in a one-hour loop that covers both sides of the river, including the Guild Hall, the old city walls, political wall murals (Nationalist as well as Unionist), cathedrals, and former shirt factories. Your ticket is good for 24 hours and also includes a 45-minute walking tour of the city walls and Bogside (£12.50, pay driver, bus departs April-Sept daily on the hour 10:00-16:00 from in front of TI and Guildhall Square, walking tour departs from from TI daily at 10:00 and 12:00, tel. 028/7137-0067, mobile 077-9116-4431, http://toptoursireland.com, info@toptoursireland.com).

Top Tours also offers trips from Derry to the Giant's Causeway and Carrick-a-Rede Rope Bridge in County Antrim (£25, runs daily May-Sept, depart TI at 11:00, return by 17:00). In addition, they offer tours to Glenveagh National Park in County Donegal (depart TI at 9:00, return by 15:00). You can book any of their tours through the Derry TI.

Self-Guided Walks

Though calm today, Derry is marked by years of tumultuous conflict. These two walks (each taking less than an hour) will increase your understanding of the town's history. The first walk, starting on the old city walls and ending at the Anglican Cathedral, focuses on Derry's early days. The second walking tour helps you easily find the city's compelling murals, which document the time of the Troubles. These tours can be done separately or linked, depending on your time.

▲▲Walk the Walls

Squatting determinedly in the city center, the old city walls of Derry (built 1613-1618 and still intact, except for wider gates to handle modern vehicles) hold an almost mythic place in Irish history.

It was here in 1688 that a group of brave apprentice boys, many of whom had been shipped to Derry as orphans after the great fire of London in 1666, made their stand. They slammed the city gates shut in the face of the approaching Catholic forces of deposed King James II. With this act, the boys galvanized the city's indecisive Protestant defenders inside the walls.

Months of negotiations and a grinding 105-day siege followed, during which a third of the 20,000 refugees and defenders crammed into the city perished. The siege was finally broken in 1689, when supply ships broke through a boom stretched across the River Foyle. The sacrifice and defiant survival of the city turned the tide in favor of newly crowned Protestant King William of Orange, who arrived in Ireland soon after and defeated James at the pivotal Battle of the Boyne.

To fully appreciate the walls, take a walk on top of them (free and open from dawn to dusk). Almost 20 feet high and at least as thick, the walls form a mile-long oval loop that you can cover in less than an hour. But the most interesting section is the half-circuit facing the Bogside, starting at Magazine Gate (stairs face the Tower Museum Derry inside the walls) and finishing at Bishop's Gate.

• *Enter the walls at Magazine Gate and find the stairs opposite the Tower Museum. Once atop the walls, head left.*

Walk the wall as it heads uphill, snaking along the earth's contours like a mini-Great Wall of China. In the row of buildings on the left (just before crossing over Castle Gate), you'll see an arch entry into the **Craft Village,** an alley lined with a cluster of cute shops and cafés that showcase the economic rejuvenation of Derry (Mon-Sat 9:30-17:30, closed Sun).

• *After crossing over Butcher Gate, stop in front of the grand building with the four columns to view the...*

First Derry Presbyterian Church: This impressive-looking building is the second church to occupy this site. The first was built by Queen Mary in the 1690s to thank the Presbyterian community for standing by their Anglican brethren during the dark days of the famous siege. That church was later torn down to make room for this stately Neoclassical, red-sandstone church finished in 1780. Over the next 200 years, time took its toll on the structure, which was eventually closed due to dry rot and Republican firebombings. But in 2011, the renovated church reopened to a chorus of cross-community approval (yet one more sign of the slow reconciliation taking place in Derry). The **Blue Coat School** exhibit behind the church highlights the important role of Presbyterians in local history (free but donation expected, May-Sept Wed-Fri 11:00-16:00, closed Sat-Tue, closed Oct-April, tel. 028/7126-1550).

• *Just up the block is the...*

Apprentice Boys Memorial Hall: Built in 1873, this houses the private lodge and meeting rooms of an all-male Protestant organization. The group is dedicated to the memory of the original 13 apprentice boys who saved the day during the 1688 siege. Each year, on the Saturday closest to the August 12 anniversary date, the modern-day Apprentice Boys Society celebrates the end of the siege with a controversial march atop the walls. These walls are considered sacred ground for devout Unionists, who claim that many who died during the famous siege were buried within the battered walls because of lack of space.

Next, you'll pass a large, square pedestal on the right atop Royal Bastion. It once supported a column in honor of Governor George Walker, the commander of the defenders during the famous siege. In 1972, the IRA blew up the column, which had 105 steps to the top (one for each day of the siege).

• *Opposite the empty pedestal is the small Anglican...*

St. Augustine Chapel: Set in a pretty graveyard, this Anglican chapel is where some believe the original sixth-century monastery of St. Columba (St. Colmcille in Irish) stood. In Victorian times, this stretch of the walls was a fashionable promenade walk.

As you walk, you'll pass a long wall (on the left)—all that's left of a **British Army base** that stood here until 2006. Two 50-foot towers used to loom out of it, bristling with cameras and listening devices. Soldiers built them here for a bird's-eye view of the once-turbulent Catholic Bogside district below. The towers' dismantlement—as well as the removal of most of the British Army from

DERRY & COUNTY DONEGAL

Derry's History

Once an island in the River Foyle, Derry (from *doire*, Irish for "oak grove") was chosen by St. Colmcille (St. Columba in English) circa A.D. 546 for a monastic settlement. He later banished himself to the island of Iona in Scotland out of remorse for sparking a bloody battle over the rights to a holy manuscript that he had secretly copied.

A thousand years later, the English defeated the last Ulster-based Gaelic chieftains in the battle of Kinsale (1601). With victory at hand, the English took advantage of the power vacuum. They began the "plantation" of Ulster with loyal Protestant subjects imported from Scotland and England. The native Irish were displaced to less desirable rocky or boggy lands, sowing the seeds of resentment that fueled the modern-day Troubles.

A dozen wealthy London guilds (grocers, haberdashers, tailors, and others) took on Derry as an investment and changed its name to "Londonderry." They built the last great walled city in Ireland to protect their investment from the surrounding—and hostile—Irish locals. The walls proved their worth in 1688-1689, when the town's Protestant defenders, loyal to King William of Orange, withstood a prolonged siege by the forces of Catholic King James II. "No surrender" is still a passionate rallying cry among Ulster Unionists determined to remain part of the United Kingdom.

The town became a major port of emigration to the New World in the early 1800s. Then, when the Industrial Revolution provided a steam-powered sewing factory, the city developed a thriving shirt-making industry. The factories here employed

Northern Ireland—is another positive sign in cautiously optimistic Derry. The walls of this former army base now contain a parking lot.

Stop at the **Double Bastion** fortified platform that occupies this corner of the city walls. The old cannon is nicknamed "Roaring Meg" for the fury of its firing during the siege.

From here, you can see across the Bogside to the not-so-far-away hills of County Donegal in the Republic. Derry was once an island, but as the River Foyle gradually changed its course, the area you see below the wall began to drain. Over time, and especially after the Great Potato Famine (1845-1849), Catholic peasants from rural Donegal began to move into Derry to find work during the mostly Catholic women who had honed their skills in rural County Donegal. Although Belfast grew larger and wealthier, Unionists tightened their grip on "Londonderry" and the walls that they regarded with almost holy reverence. In 1921, they insisted that the city be included in Northern Ireland when the province was partitioned from the new Irish Free State (later to become the Republic of Ireland). A bit of gerrymandering (with three lightly populated Unionist districts outvoting two densely populated Nationalist districts) ensured that the Protestant minority maintained control of the city, despite its Catholic majority.

Derry was a key escort base for US convoys headed for Britain during World War II, and 60 surviving German U-boats were instructed to surrender here at the end of the war. After the war, poor Catholics—unable to find housing—took over the abandoned military barracks, with multiple families living in each dwelling. Only homeowners were allowed to vote, and the Unionist minority, which controlled city government, was not eager to build more housing that would tip the voting balance away from them. Over the years, sectarian pressures gradually built—until they reached the boiling point. The ugly events of Bloody Sunday on January 30, 1972, brought worldwide attention to the Troubles (for more details, see "Bloody Sunday" sidebar on page 72).

Today, life has stabilized in Derry, and the population has increased by 25 percent in the last 30 years, to about 85,000. The modern Foyleside Shopping Centre, bankrolled by investors from Boston, opened in 1995. The 1998 Good Friday Peace Accord has provided significant progress toward peace, and the British Army withdrew 90 percent of its troops in mid-2007. With a population that is 70 percent Catholic, the city has agreed to alternate Nationalist and Unionist mayors. There is a feeling of cautious optimism as Derry—the epicenter of bombs and bloody conflicts in the 1960s and 1970s—now boasts a history museum that airs all viewpoints.

DERRY & COUNTY DONEGAL

Industrial Revolution. They settled on this least desirable land...on the soggy bog side of the city.

Directly below and to the right are **Free Derry Corner** and **Rossville Street,** where the tragic events of Bloody Sunday took place in 1972. Down on the left is the 18th-century **Long Tower** Catholic church, named after the monk-built round tower that once stood in the area.

• *Head to the grand brick building behind you. This is the...*

Verbal Arts Centre: A former Presbyterian school, this center promotes the development of local literary arts in the form of poetry, drama, writing, and storytelling. You can drop in for a cup of coffee in Bloom's Cafe and see what performances might be on during your visit (Mon-Thu 9:00-17:30, Fri 9:00-16:00, closed Sat-Sun, tel. 028/7126-6946, www.verbalartscentre.co.uk).

• *Go left another 50 yards around the corner to reach...*

Bishop's Gate: From here, look up Bishop Street Within (inside the walls). This was the site of another British Army surveil-lance tower. Placed just inside the town walls, it overlooked the neighborhood until 2006. Now look in the other direction to see Bishop Street Without (outside the walls). You'll spot a modern wall topped by a high mesh fence, running along the left side of Bishop Street Without. This is a so-called **"peace wall,"** built to ensure the security of the Protestant en-

clave living behind it in Derry's Fountain neighborhood. When the Troubles reignited 45 years ago, 20,000 Protestants lived on this side of the river. Sadly, this small housing development of 1,000 people is all that remains of that proud community today. The rest have chosen to move across the river to the mostly Protestant Waterside district. The stone tower halfway down the "peace wall" is all that remains of the old jail that briefly held doomed rebel Wolfe Tone after the 1798 revolt against the British.

• *From Bishop's Gate, those short on time can descend from the walls and walk 15 minutes directly back through the heart of the old city, along Bishop Street Within and Shipquay Street to Guildhall Square. With more time, consider visiting St. Columb's Cathedral, the Long Tower Church, and the murals of the Bogside.*

▲▲Bogside Murals Walk

The Catholic Bogside area was the tinderbox of the modern Troubles in Northern Ireland. Bloody Sunday, a terrible confrontation during a march that occurred more than 40 years ago, sparked a sectarian inferno, and the ashes have not yet fully cooled. Today, the murals of the Bogside give visitors an accessible glimpse of this community's passionate perception of those events.

The events are memorialized in 12 **murals** painted on the ends of residential flats along a 300-yard stretch of Rossville Street and Lecky Road, where the march took place. You can reach them from Waterloo Place via William Street, from the old city walls at Butcher Gate via the long set of stairs extending below Fahan Street on the grassy hillside, or by the stairs leading down from the Long Tower Church. These days, this neighborhood is gritty but quiet and safe, and the murals are even lit up at night.

Two brothers, Tom and William Kelly, and their childhood friend Kevin Hasson are known as the Bogside Artists. They grew

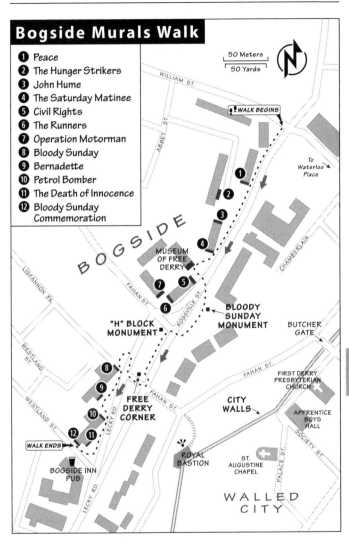

Bogside Murals Walk

1 Peace
2 The Hunger Strikers
3 John Hume
4 The Saturday Matinee
5 Civil Rights
6 The Runners
7 Operation Motorman
8 Bloody Sunday
9 Bernadette
10 Petrol Bomber
11 The Death of Innocence
12 Bloody Sunday Commemoration

50 Meters
50 Yards

WILLIAM ST.

WALK BEGINS

ABBEY ST.

To Waterloo Place

BOGSIDE

CHAMBERLAIN

MUSEUM OF FREE DERRY

LISFANNON PK.

FAHAN ST.

ROSSVILLE ST.

BLOODY SUNDAY MONUMENT

BUTCHER GATE

"H" BLOCK MONUMENT

WESTLAND ST.

FAHAN ST.

FIRST DERRY PRESBYTERIAN CHURCH

FREE DERRY CORNER

CITY WALLS

WESTLAND ST.

LECKY RD.

FAHAN ST.

APPRENTICE BOYS HALL

SOCIETY ST.

WALK ENDS

BOGSIDE INN PUB

LECKY RD.

ROYAL BASTION

ST. AUGUSTINE CHAPEL

PALACE ST.

WALLED CITY

DERRY & COUNTY DONEGAL

up in the Bogside and witnessed the tragic events that took place there, which led them to begin painting the murals in 1994. One of the brothers, Tom, gained a reputation as a "heritage mural" painter, specializing in scenes of life in the old days. In a surprising and hopeful development, Tom was later invited into Derry's Protestant Fountain neighborhood to work with a youth club there on three proud heritage murals that were painted over paramilitary graffiti. For more about this unique trio, visit their website—www.bogsideartists.com.

DERRY & COUNTY DONEGAL

Bloody Sunday

Inspired by civil rights marches in America in the mid-1960s, and the Prague Spring uprising and Paris student strikes of 1968, civil rights groups began to protest in Northern Ireland. Initially, their goals were to gain better housing, secure fair voting rights, and end employment discrimination for Catholics in the North. Tensions mounted, and clashes with the predominantly Protestant Royal Ulster Constabulary police force became frequent. Eventually, the British Army was called in to keep the peace.

On January 30, 1972, about 10,000 people protesting internment without trial held an illegal march sponsored by the Northern Ireland Civil Rights Association. British Army barricades kept them from the center of Derry, so they marched through the Bogside neighborhood.

That afternoon, some youths rioted on the fringe of the march. An elite parachute regiment had orders to move in and make arrests in the Rossville Street area. Shooting broke out, and after 25 minutes, 13 marchers were dead and 13 were wounded (one of the wounded later died). The soldiers claimed they came under attack from gunfire and nail-bombs. The marchers said the army shot indiscriminately at unarmed civilians.

The tragic clash, called "Bloody Sunday," led to a dramatic increase in Nationalism and a flood of fresh IRA volunteers. An investigation at the time exonerated the soldiers, but the relatives of the victims called it a whitewash and insisted on their innocence.

In 1998, then-British Prime Minister Tony Blair promised a new inquiry, which became the longest and most expensive in British legal history. In 2010, a 12-year investigation—the Saville Report—determined that the Bloody Sunday civil rights protesters were innocent and called the deaths of 14 protesters unjustified.

In a dramatic 2010 speech in the House of Commons, British Prime Minister David Cameron apologized to the people of Derry. "What happened on Bloody Sunday was both unjustified and unjustifiable. It was wrong," he declared. Cheers rang out in Derry's Guildhall Square, where thousands had gathered to watch the speech on a video screen. After 38 years of struggle, Northern Ireland's bloodiest wound started healing.

The Walk: Start out at the corner of Rossville and William streets.

The Bogside murals face different directions (and some are partially hidden by buildings), so they're not all visible from a single viewpoint. Plan on walking three long blocks along Rossville Street (which becomes Lecky Road) to see them all. Residents are used to visitors and don't mind if you photograph the murals.

From William Street, walk south along the right side of Rossville Street toward Free Derry Corner. The murals will all be on your right.

The first mural you'll walk past is the colorful ❶ *Peace,* showing the silhouette of a dove in flight (left side of mural) and an oak leaf (right side of mural), both created from a single ribbon. A peace campaign asked Derry city schoolchildren to write suggestions for positive peacetime images; their words inspired this artwork. The dove is a traditional symbol of peace, and the oak leaf is a traditional symbol of Derry—recognized by both communities. The dove flies from the sad blue of the past toward the warm yellow of the future.

Next, ❷ *The Hunger Strikers* features two long-haired figures wearing blankets. This mural represents the IRA prisoners who re-

fused to wear the uniforms of common criminal inmates—an attempt to force the British to treat them instead as legitimate political prisoners (who were allowed to wear their own clothes). The giant red letter *H* looms behind them, a symbol of the H-block layout of Maze Prison near Belfast.

Smaller and easy to miss (above a ramp with banisters) is ❸ *John Hume.* It's actually a collection of four faces (clockwise from upper left): Nationalist leader John Hume, Martin Luther King Jr., Nelson Mandela, and Mother Teresa. The Brooklyn Bridge in the middle symbolizes the long-term bridges of understanding that the work of these four Nobel Peace Prize-winning activists created. Born in the Bogside, Hume still maintains a home here.

Now look for ❹ *The Saturday Matinee,* which depicts an outgunned but undaunted local youth behind a screen shield. He holds a stone, ready to throw, while a British armored vehicle approaches (echoing the famous Tiananmen Square photo of the lone Chinese man facing the tank). Why *Saturday Matinee?* It's because the weekend was the best time for locals to "have a go at" the army; people were off work and youths were out of school.

Nearby is ❺ *Civil Rights,* showing a marching Derry crowd carrying an anti-sectarian banner. It dates from the days when Martin Luther King Jr.'s successful nonviolent marches were being seen worldwide on TV, creating a dramatic, global ripple effect. Civil

Political Murals

The dramatic and emotional murals you'll encounter in Northern Ireland will likely be one of the enduring travel memories that you'll take home with you.

During the 19th century, Protestant neighborhoods hung flags and streamers each July to commemorate the victory of King William of Orange at the Battle of the Boyne in 1690. Modern murals evolved from these colorful annual displays. With the advent of industrial paints, temporary seasonal displays became permanent territorial statements.

Unionist murals were created during the extended Home Rule political debate that eventually led to the partitioning of the island in 1921 and the creation of Northern Ireland. Murals that expressed opposing views in Nationalist Catholic neighborhoods were outlawed. The ban remained until the eruption of the modern Troubles, when staunchly Nationalist Catholic communities isolated themselves behind barricades, eluding state control and gaining freedom to express their pent-up passions. In Derry, this form of symbolic, cultural, and ideological resistance first appeared in 1969 with the simple "You are now entering Free Derry" message that you'll still see painted on the surviving gable wall at Free Derry Corner.

Found mostly in working-class neighborhoods of Belfast and Derry, today's political murals have become a dynamic form of popular culture. They blur the line between art and propaganda, giving visitors a striking glimpse of each community's history, identity, and values.

rights marches, inspired by King and using the same methods to combat a similar set of grievances, gave this long-suffering community a powerful new voice.

In the building behind this mural, you'll find the small but intense **Museum of Free Derry** (£3, Mon-Fri 9:30-16:30 year-round, April-Sept also Sat 13:00-16:00, July-Sept also Sun 13:00-16:00, 55 Glenfada Park, tel. 028/7136-0880, www.museumoffreederry. org). Photos, shirts with bullet holes, and a 45-minute video documentary convey the painful experience of the people of the Bogside during the worst of the Troubles.

Cross over to the other side of Rossville Street to see the **Bloody Sunday Monument.**

This small, fenced-off stone obelisk lists the names of those who died that day, most within 50 yards of this spot. Take a look at the map pedestal by the monument, which shows how a rubble barricade was erected to block the street. A 10-story housing project called Rossville Flats stood here in those days. After peaceful protests failed (with Bloody Sunday being the watershed event), Nationalist youths became more aggressive. British troops were wary of being hit by Molotov cocktails thrown from the rooftop of the housing project.

Cross back again, this time over to the grassy median strip that runs down the middle of Rossville Street. At this end stands a granite letter *H* inscribed with the names of the 10 IRA hunger strikers who died in the H-block of Maze Prison in 1981. The prison was closed after the release of all prisoners (both Unionist and Nationalist) in 2000.

From here, as you look across at the corner of Fahan Street, you get a good view of two murals. In ❻ *The Runners* (right), three rioting youths flee tear gas from canisters used by the British Army to disperse hostile crowds. More than 1,000 canisters were used during the Battle of the Bogside; "nonlethal" rubber bullets killed 17 people over the course of the Troubles. Meanwhile, in ❼ *Operation Motorman* (left), a soldier wields a sledgehammer to break through a house door, depicting the massive push by the British Army to open up the Bogside's barricaded "no-go" areas that the IRA had controlled for three years (1969-1972).

Walk down to the other end of the median strip where the white wall of **Free Derry Corner** announces "You are now entering Free Derry" (imitating a similarly defiant slogan of the time in once-isolated West Berlin). This was the gabled end of a string of houses that stood here over 40 years ago. During the Troubles, it became a traditional meeting place for speakers to address crowds.

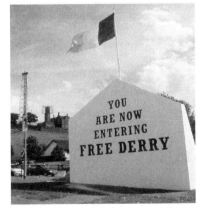

Cross back to the right side of the street (now Lecky Road) to see ❽ *Bloody Sunday,* in which a small group of men carry a body from that ill-fated march. It's based on a famous photo of Father Edward Daly that was taken that terrible day. Hunched over, he waves a white handkerchief to request safe passage in order to evacuate a mortally wounded protester. The bloodstained civil rights banner was inserted under the soldier's feet for extra emphasis. After Bloody Sunday, the previously marginal IRA suddenly found itself swamped with bitterly determined young recruits.

Near it is a mural called ❾ *Bernadette.* The woman with the megaphone is Bernadette Devlin McAliskey, an outspoken civil rights leader, who at age 21 became the youngest elected member of British Parliament. Behind her kneels a female supporter, banging a trash-can lid against the street in a traditional expression of protest in Nationalist neighborhoods. Trash-can lids were also used to warn neighbors of the approach of British patrols.

❿ *Petrol Bomber,* showing a teen wearing an army-surplus gas mask, captures the Battle of the Bogside, when locals barricaded their community, effectively shutting out British rule. Though the main figure's face is obscured by the mask, his body clearly communicates the resolve of an oppressed people. In the background, the long-gone Rossville Flats housing project still looms, with an Irish tricolor flag flying from its top.

In ⓫ *The Death of Innocence,* a young girl stands in front of bomb wreckage. She is Annette McGavigan, a 14-year-old who was killed on this corner by crossfire in 1971. She was the 100th fatality of the Troubles, which eventually took more than 3,000 lives (and she was also a cousin of one of the artists). The broken gun beside her points to the ground, signifying that it's no longer being wielded. The large butterfly above her shoulder symbolizes the hope for peace. For years, the artists left the butterfly an empty silhouette until they felt confident that the peace process had succeeded. They finally filled in the butterfly with optimistic colors in the summer of 2006.

Finally, around the corner, you'll see a circle of male faces.

This mural, painted in 1997 to observe the 25th anniversary of the tragedy, is called ⓬ *Bloody Sunday Commemoration* and shows the 14 victims. They are surrounded by a ring of 14 oak leaves—the symbol of Derry. When relatives of the dead learned that the three Bogside Artists were beginning to paint this mural, many came forward to loan the artists precious photos of their loved ones, so they could be more accurately depicted.

Across the street, drop into the **Bogside Inn** for a beverage and check out the black-and-white photos of events in the area during the Troubles. This pub has been here through it all, and lives on to tell the tale.

While these murals preserve the struggles of the late 20th century, today sectarian violence has given way to negotiations and a settlement that seems to be working. The British apology for the Bloody Sunday shootings was a huge step forward. Nationalist leader John Hume (who shared the 1998 Nobel Peace Prize with Unionist leader David Trimble) once borrowed a quote from Gandhi to explain his nonviolent approach to the peace process: "An eye for an eye leaves everyone blind."

Sights in Derry

▲▲Tower Museum Derry

Housed in a modern reconstruction of a fortified medieval tower house that belonged to the local O'Doherty clan, this well-organized museum provides an excellent introduction to the city. Combining modern audiovisual displays with historical artifacts, the exhibits tell the story of the city from a skillfully unbiased viewpoint, sorting out some of the tangled historical roots of Northern Ireland's Troubles.

Cost and Hours: £4.20; June-Aug Mon-Sat 10:00-16:30, closed Sun; Sept-May Tue-Sat 10:00-16:30, closed Sun-Mon; free audioguide for Armada exhibits, Union Hall Place, tel. 028/7137-2411.

Visiting the Museum: The museum is divided into two sections: the Story of Derry (on the ground floor) and the Spanish Armada (on the four floors of the tower).

Start with the **Story of Derry,** which explains the city's monastic origins 1,500 years ago. It moves through pivotal events, such as the 1688-1689 siege, as well as unexpected blips, like Amelia Earhart's emergency landing. Don't miss the thought-provoking 15-minute film in the small theater—it offers an evenhanded local perspective on the tragic events of the modern sectarian conflict, giving you a better handle on what makes this unique city tick. Scan the displays of paramilitary paraphernalia in the hallway lined with colored curbstones—red, white, and blue Union Jack colors for Unionists; and the green, white, and orange Irish tricolor for Nationalists.

The tower section holds the **Spanish Armada** exhibits, filled with items taken from the wreck of *La Trinidad Valencera*. It sank in fierce storms nicknamed the "Protestant Winds" off the coast of Donegal in 1588. A third of the Armada's ships were lost in storms off the coasts of Ireland and Scotland. Survivors who made it ashore were hunted and killed by English soldiers. But a small number made it to Dunluce Castle, where the sympathetic lord, who was no friend of the English, smuggled them to Scotland and eventual freedom in France.

Guild Hall

This Neo-Gothic building, complete with clock tower, is the ceremonial seat of city government. It first opened in 1890 on re-

claimed lands that were once the mudflats of the River Foyle. Destroyed by fire and rebuilt in 1913, it was massively damaged by IRA bombs in 1972. In an ironic twist, Gerry Doherty, one of those convicted of the bombings, was elected as a member of the Derry City Council a dozen years later. In November of 1995, US President Bill Clinton spoke to thousands who packed into Guildhall Square. Inside the hall are the Council Chamber, party offices, and an assembly hall featuring stained-glass windows showing scenes from Derry history. Take an informational pamphlet from the front window and explore, if civic and cultural events are not taking place inside.

Cost and Hours: Free, Mon-Fri 9:00-17:30, closed Sat-Sun, tel. 028/7137-7335, www.derrycity.gov.uk/guildhall.

Peace Bridge Stroll

A stroll across the architecturally fetching Peace Bridge rewards you with great views as you look back west across the river toward the city center. The €14 million pedestrian Peace Bridge opened in 2011, linking neighborhoods long divided by the river. On the far side, the former Ebrington Barracks British Army base (1841-2003) sits on prime real estate and surrounds a huge square that was once the military parade ground. This area will eventually be developed with a hotel, restaurant, and museum complex. The slope down to the river has been dubbed "Mute Meadows," where 40 pillars will be lit up at night with shifting colors. The site has already become an outdoor concert venue and gathering place for the whole community.

Hands Across the Divide

Designed by local teacher Maurice Harron after the fall of the Iron Curtain, this powerful metal sculpture of two figures extending their hands to each other was inspired by the growing hope for peace and reconciliation in Northern Ireland (located in a roundabout at the west end of Craigavon Bridge).

The Tillie and Henderson's shirt factory

(opened in 1857 and burned down in 2003) once stood on the banks of the river beside the bridge, looming over the figures. In its heyday, Derry's shirt industry employed more than 15,000 workers (90 percent of whom were women) in sweathouses typical of the human toll of the Industrial Revolution. Karl Marx mentioned this factory in *Das Kapital* as an example of women's transition from domestic to industrial work lives.

St. Columb's Cathedral

Marked by the tall spire inside the walls, this Anglican cathedral was built from 1628 to 1633 in a style called "Planter's Gothic." Its construction was financed by the same London companies that backed the Protestant plantation of Londonderry. It was the first Protestant cathedral built in Britain after the Reformation, and the cathedral played an important part in the defense of the city during the siege. During that time, cannons were mounted on its roof, and the original spire was scavenged for lead to melt into cannon shot.

Cost and Hours: £2 donation, Mon-Sat 9:00-17:00, closed Sun, tel. 028/7126-7313, www.stcolumbscathedral.org.

Visiting the Church: Before you enter, walk over to the "Heroes' Mound" at the end of the churchyard closest to the town wall. Underneath this grassy dome is a mass grave of some of those who died during the 1689 siege.

In the cathedral entryway, you'll find a hollow cannonball that was lobbed into the city—it contained the besiegers' surrender terms. Inside, along the nave, hangs a musty collection of battle flags and Union Jacks that once inspired troops during the siege, the Crimean War, and World War II. The American flag hangs among them, from the time when the first GIs to enter the European theater in World War II were based in Northern Ireland. Check out the small chapter-house museum in the back of the church to see the original locks of the gates of Derry and more relics of the siege.

Long Tower Church

Built below the walls on the hillside above the Bogside, this modest-looking church is worth a visit for its stunning high altar. The name comes from a stone monastic round tower that stood here for centuries but was dismantled and used for building materials in the 1600s. Long Tower Church, the oldest Catholic church in Derry, was finished in 1786, during a time of enlightened relations between the city's two religious communities. Protestant Bishop Hervey gave a generous-for-the-time £200 donation and had the four Corinthian columns shipped in from Naples to frame the Neo-Renaissance altar.

Hidden outside, behind the church and facing the Bogside, is a simple shrine beneath a hawthorn tree. It marks the spot where outlawed Masses were secretly held before this church was built, during the infamous Penal Law period of the early 1700s. Through the Penal Laws, the English attempted to weaken Catholicism's influence by banishing priests and forbidding Catholics from buying land, attending school, voting, and holding office.

Cost and Hours: Free, generally open Mon-Sat 7:30-20:30, Sun 7:30-19:00—depending on available staff and church functions, tel. 028/7126-2301, www.longtowerchurch.org.

Nightlife in Derry

The **Millennium Forum** is a modern venue that reflects the city's revived investment in local culture, concerts, and plays (box office open Mon-Sat 9:30-17:30, inside city walls on Newmarket Street near Ferryquay Gate, tel. 028/7126-4455, www.millenniumforum.co.uk, boxoffice@millenniumforum.co.uk).

The **Nerve Centre** shows a wide variety of art-house films and live concerts (inside city walls at 7-8 Magazine Street, near Butcher Gate, tel. 028/7126-0562, www.nervecentre.org).

The **Playhouse Theatre** is an intimate venue for plays (£9-20 tickets, inside the walls on Artillery Street, between New Gate and Ferryquay Gate, tel. 028/7126-8027, www.derryplayhouse.co.uk).

If you want to get away from tourists and mingle with Derry residents, try **Peadar O'Donnell's** pub on Waterloo Street for Derry's best nightly traditional music sessions (often starts late, at 23:00; 53 Waterloo Street, tel. 028/7137-2318).

Sleeping in Derry

$$$ Tower Hotel is the only hotel actually inside Derry's historic walls. It's a real splurge, with 93 modern and immaculate rooms, a classy bistro restaurant, and private basement parking (Sb-£65-99, Db-£70-135, online deals, Butcher Street, tel. 028/7137-1000, www.towerhotelderry.com, reservations@thd.ie).

$$ Merchant's House, on a quiet street a 10-minute stroll from Waterloo Place, is a fine Georgian townhouse with a grand, colorful drawing room and nine rooms sporting marble fireplaces and ornate plasterwork (S-£40-55, Sb-£60-75, Db-£65-80, Tb-£90-110, Qb-£100-135, Wi-Fi, 16 Queen Street, tel. 028/7126-9691, www.thesaddlershouse.com, saddlershouse@btinternet.com, Joan and Peter Pyne also run the Saddler's House, next). Ask the Pynes about their appealing self-catering townhouse rentals inside the walls (great for families or anyone needing extra space).

$$ Saddler's House, run by the owners of Merchant's House, is a charming Victorian townhouse with seven rooms located a couple of blocks closer to the old town walls (S-£40-55, Sb-£55-

---

Sleep Code

(£1 = about $1.60, country code: 44, area code: 028)
S = Single, **D** = Double/Twin, **T** = Triple, **Q** = Quad, **b** = bathroom, **s** = shower only. Breakfast is included and credit cards are accepted unless otherwise noted.

To help you easily sort through these listings, I've divided the accommodations into three categories, based on the price for a standard double room with bath:

$$$ Higher Priced—Most rooms £80 or more.

$$ Moderately Priced—Most rooms between £40-80.

$ Lower Priced—Most rooms £40 or less.

Prices can change without notice; verify the hotel's current rates online or by email. For the best prices, always book direct.

70, Db-£60-75, Wi-Fi, 36 Great James Street, tel. 028/7126-9691, www.thesaddlershouse.com, saddlershouse@btinternet.com).

$$ Travelodge has 44 comfortable rooms, a great location, and a handy adjacent parking garage—but beware of large, loud party groups on weekends (Db-£55 Sun-Thu, Db-£65-80 Fri-Sat, occasional online discounts if you book ahead, continental breakfast-£7, 22-24 Strand Road, tel. 028/7127-1271, www.travelodge. ie).

$ Paddy's Palace Hostel rents 40 decent beds for £12-15 a night with breakfast. Look for the green-and-beige building, and pause to read the great Mark Twain quote above the front door (4-6 beds/room, family rooms with private bathroom for up to four-£50, guest computer, laundry facilities, kitchen, 1 Woodleigh Terrace, Asylum Road, tel. 028/7130-9051, www.paddyspalace. com, steve@irishexperience.ie, Stephen McPhilemy). They also have a couple of self-catering apartments nearby, and Stephen offers walking tours (see "Tours in Derry," earlier).

Eating in Derry

The **Custom House Restaurant & Wine Bar** is the classiest place in town, serving great £14-19 meals and a selection of fine wines in a posh, calm space. It faces the river half a block from the Guild Hall (Mon-Sat 12:00-14:30 & 17:30-21:30, Sun 15:00-21:00, Queens Quay, tel. 028/7137-3366).

The hip, trendy **Exchange Restaurant and Wine Bar** offers £7-10 lunches and quality £12-16 dinners with flair, in a central location near the river behind Waterloo Place (Mon-Sat 12:00-14:30 & 17:30-22:00, Sun 16:00-21:00, Queen's Quay, tel. 028/7127-3990).

Mandarin Palace dishes up good £10-15 Chinese dinners in a crisp dining room facing the river (Mon-Fri 12:00-14:30 & 16:30-23:00, Sat 16:30-23:00, Sun 13:00-22:00, weekday buffet lunch, £10 two-course early-bird deals 16:30-19:00, Queens Quay at Lower Clarendon Street, tel. 028/7137-3656).

Easygoing **Fitzroy's,** tucked below Ferryquay Gate, serves good £9-12 lunches and £12-19 dinners (Mon-Sat 12:00-22:00, Sun 13:00-20:00, 2-4 Bridge Street, tel. 028/7126-6211).

Austins Department Store, right on the Diamond in the center of the old city, is Ireland's oldest department store (1830). It predates Harrods in London by 15 years, and Macy's in New York by 25 years. Its basic top-floor café comes with lofty views and £5.50 lunch specials (Mon-Sat 9:30-17:30, Sun 13:00-17:00, 2-6 The Diamond, tel. 028/7126-1817).

Bloom's Cafe, a cheap and cheery basic lunch option, hides inside the Verbal Arts Centre atop the walls near Double Bastion (Mon-Fri 9:00-16:00, closed Sat-Sun, tel. 028/7127-2517).

Supermarkets: **Tesco** has everything for picnics and road munchies (Mon-Fri 8:00-21:00, Sat 8:00-20:00, Sun 13:00-18:00, corner of Strand Road and Clarendon Street). **SuperValu** meets the same needs (Mon-Wed and Sat 8:30-19:00, Thu-Fri 8:30-20:00, Sun 12:30-17:30, Waterloo Place).

Derry Connections

From Derry, it's an hour's drive to Portrush. If you're using public transportation, consider spending £16.50 for a Zone 4 iLink smartcard (£15 top-up for each additional day), good for all-day train and bus use in Northern Ireland. Translink has useful updated schedules and prices for both trains and buses in Northern Ireland (tel. 028/9066-6630, www.translink.co.uk). Keep in mind that some bus and train schedules, road signs, and maps may say "Londonderry" or "L'Derry" instead of "Derry."

From Derry by Train to: Portrush (8/day, 1.5 hours, change in Coleraine), **Belfast** (8/day, 2.5 hours), **Dublin** (6/day, 5 hours).

By Bus to: Galway (6/day, 5.5 hours), **Portrush** (5/day, 1.25 hours, change in Coleraine), **Belfast** (hourly, 1.75 hours), **Dublin** (12/day, 4.5 hours).

Between Derry and Galway

If you're driving into Northern Ireland from Galway, Westport, or Strokestown and don't have time to explore Donegal, consider these two interesting stops in the interior.

Belleek Pottery Visitors Centre

Just over the Northern Ireland border (30 miles/48 km northeast of Sligo) is the cute town of Belleek, famous for its pottery. The Belleek Parian China factory welcomes visitors with a small gallery and museum, a 20-minute video, a cheery cafeteria, and fascinating 30-minute guided tours of its working factory. Crazed shoppers who forget to fill out a VAT refund form will find their finances looking Belleek.

Cost and Hours: Free, £4 tours, visitors center open March-Sept Mon-Fri 9:00-17:30, Sat 10:00-17:30, Sun 14:00-17:30; longer hours July-Sept, shorter hours Oct-Feb; closed Sat Jan-Feb; closed Sun Nov-Feb; no tours Sat-Sun; call to confirm tour schedule and reserve a spot, tel. 028/6865-8501, www.belleek.ie.

▲Ulster American Folk Park

North of Omagh (five miles/8 km on A-5), this combination museum and folk park commemorates the many Irish who left their homeland during the hard times of the 19th century. Exhibits show life before emigration, on the boat, and in America. You'll gain insight into the origins of the tough Scots-Irish stock—think Davy Crockett (his people were from Derry) and Andrew Jackson (Carrickfergus roots)—who later shaped America's westward migration. You'll also find good coverage of the *Titanic* tragedy, and its effect on the Ulster folk who built the ship and the loved ones it left behind.

Cost and Hours: £6.50; March-Sept Tue-Sun 10:00-17:00; Oct-Feb Tue-Fri 10:00-16:00, Sat-Sun 11:00-16:00; closed Mon year-round; cafeteria, 2 Mellon Road, tel. 028/8224-3292, www.nmni.com.

Nearby: The adjacent **Mellon Centre for Migration Studies** is handy for genealogy searches (Mon-Fri 10:30-17:00, closed Sat-Sun, tel. 028/8225-6315, www.qub.ac.uk/cms).

County Donegal

Donegal is the most remote (and perhaps the most ruggedly beautiful) county in Ireland. It's not on the way to anywhere, and it wears its isolation well. With more native Irish speakers than in any other county, the old ways are better preserved here. The northernmost part of Ireland, Donegal remains connected to the Republic by a slim, five-mile-wide umbilical cord of land on its southern coast. It's also Ireland's second-biggest county, with a wide-open "big sky" interior and a shattered-glass, 200-mile, jagged coastline of islands and inlets.

This is the home turf of St. Colmcille (St. Columba in English; means "dove of the church" in Irish), who was born here in 521. In the hierarchy of revered Irish saints, he's second only to St. Patrick. A proud Gaelic culture held out in Donegal to the bitter end, when the O'Donnells and the O'Dohertys, the two most famous local clans, were finally defeated by the English in the early 1600s. After their defeat, the region became known as Dun na nGall ("the fort of the foreigner"), which was eventually anglicized to Donegal.

As the English moved in, four Donegal-dwelling friars (certain that Gaelic ways would be lost forever) painstakingly wrote down Irish history from Noah's Ark to their present. This labor of love became known as the Annals of the Four Masters, and without it, much of our knowledge of early Irish history and myth would have been lost. An obelisk stands in their honor in the main square of Donegal town.

The hardy people of County Donegal have come out on the short end of the modern technology stick. They were famous for their quality tweed weaving, a cottage industry that has gradually given way to modern industrial production in far-off cities. A small but energetic Irish fishing fleet still churns offshore—in the wake of larger EU factory ships poaching traditionally Irish waters (see "Irish Fishermen Feel the Squeeze," later).

But culturally, the county shines. The traditional Irish musicians of Donegal play a driving style of music with a distinctively fast and forceful rhythm. Meanwhile, Enya (local Gweedore gal made good) has crafted languid, ethereal tunes that glide from mood to mood. Both *Dancing at Lughnasa* and *The Secret of Roan Inish* were filmed in County Donegal. Today, emigration has taken its toll, and the region relies on a trickle of tourism spilling over from Northern Ireland.

Orientation to County Donegal

Remember, you are leaving the UK for the Republic of Ireland. Once you cross into the Republic, all currency is in euros, not pounds. For B&B rates, entry fees, and all other costs in Donegal, keep this exchange rate in mind: €1 = about $1.30. Long-distance dialing is different too. To call Northern Ireland from the Republic of Ireland, dial 048 and then the local eight-digit number. To call the Republic of Ireland from Northern Ireland, dial 00-353, then the area code without its initial 0, and finally the local number.

Self-Guided Driving Tour

Donegal Loop Trip

Here's my choice for a scenic mix of Donegal highlands and coastal views, organized as a daylong circuit (240 km/150 miles) for drivers based across the border in Derry. If you're coming north from Galway or Westport, you could incorporate parts of this drive into your itinerary.

Route Summary: Drive west out of Derry (direction: Letterkenny) on Buncrana Road, which becomes A-2 (and then N-13 across the border in the Republic). Follow the signs into Letterkenny, and take R-250 out the other (west) end of town. Veer right (north) onto R-251, and stay on it through Church Hill, all the way across the highlands, until you link up with N-56 approaching Bunbeg. After a couple of kilometers on N-56, take R-258 from Gweedore; it's another six kilometers (four miles) into Bunbeg. Depart Bunbeg going north on R-257, around Bloody Foreland, and rejoin N-56 near Gortahork. Take N-56 through Dunfanaghy (possible Horn Head mini-loop option here) and then south, back into Letterkenny. Retrace your route from Letterkenny via N-13 and A-2 back into Derry.

Driving Tips: An early start and an Ordnance Survey atlas are essential. It's cheapest to top off your gas tank in Letterkenny. Consider bringing along a picnic lunch to enjoy from a scenic roadside pullout along the Bloody Foreland R-257 road, or out on the Horn Head loop. Bring your camera and remember—not all who wander are lost.

The sights along this route are well-marked. Don't underestimate the time it takes to get around here, as the narrow roads are full of curves and bumps. Dogs, bred to herd sheep, dart from side lanes to practice their bluffing techniques on their reflections in your hubcaps. If you average 65 kilometers per hour (about 40 mph) over the course of the day, you've got a very good suspension system. Folks wanting to linger at more than a couple of sights will need to slow down and consider an overnight stop in Dunfanaghy.

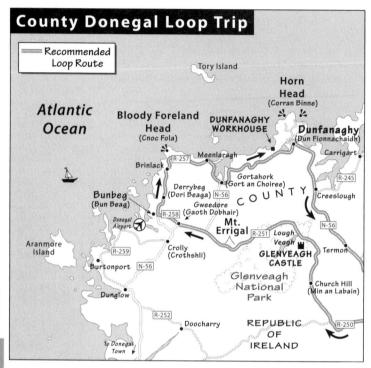

County Donegal Loop Trip

Recommended
Loop Route

Tory Island

Atlantic Ocean

Horn Head
(Corran Binne)

Bloody Foreland Head
(Cnoc Fola)

DUNFANAGHY WORKHOUSE

Dunfanaghy
(Dún Fionnachaidh)

Carrigart

R-257   Meenlaragh

Brinlack

Gortahork
(Gort an Choiree)

R-245

Derrybeg
(Dori Beaga)   N-56

Creeslough

Bunbeg
(Bun Beag)

Gweedore
(Gaoth Dobhair)

C O U N T Y

R-258

Donegal Airport

Mt. Errigal   R-251   Lough Veagh

N-56

Aranmore Island

R-259   Crolly
(Crothshli)

GLENVEAGH CASTLE

Termon

Burtonport   N-56

Glenveagh National Park

Church Hill
(Min an Labain)

Dunglow

R-252

Doocharry

REPUBLIC OF IRELAND

R-250

To Donegal Town

DERRY & COUNTY DONEGAL

The Tour Begins

• *Leave Derry on A-2, which becomes N-13 near the town of Bridge End. You'll see a sign for the* Grianan Aileach Ring Fort *posted on N-13, not far from the junction with R-239. Turn up the steep hill at the modern church with the round roof, and follow signs three kilometers (2 miles) to find...*

▲Grianan Aileach Ring Fort

This dramatic, ancient ring fort perches on an 800-foot hill just inside the Republic, a stone's throw from Derry. It's an Iron Age fortification, built about the time of Christ, and was once the royal stronghold of the O'Neill clan, which dominated Ulster for centuries. Its stout dry-stone walls (no mortar) are 12 feet thick and 18 feet high, creating an interior sanctuary 80 feet in diameter (entry is free and unattended).

Once inside, you can scramble up the stairs, which are built

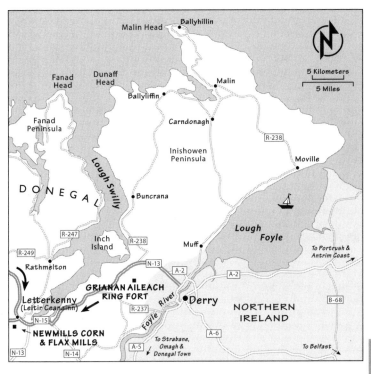

into the walls, to enjoy panoramic views in all directions. Murtagh O'Brien, King of Desmond (roughly, today's Limerick, Clare, and Tipperary counties), destroyed the fort in 1101...the same power-play year in which he gave the Rock of Cashel to the Church. He had each of his soldiers carry away one stone, attempting to make it tougher for the O'Neill clan to find the raw materials to rebuild. What you see today is mostly a reconstruction from the 1870s.

• *Return to N-13 and head to and through Letterkenny, continuing out the other (west) end of town on R-250. Eight kilometers (5 miles) west of Letterkenny on this road, you'll reach the...*

Newmills Corn and Flax Mills

Come here for a glimpse of the 175-year-old Industrial Revolution, shown high-tech Ulster style. Linen, which comes from flax, was king in this region. The 15-minute film does a nifty job of explaining the process, showing how the common flax plant ends up as cloth. Working in a mill sounds like a mellow job, but conditions were noisy, unhealthy, and exhausting. Veteran mill workers often braved respiratory disease, deafness, lost fingers, and extreme fire danger. For their trouble, they usually got to keep about 10 percent of what they milled.

The corn mill is still in working condition but requires a skilled miller to operate it. This mill ground oats—"corn" means oats in

Ireland. (What we call corn, they call maize.) The huge waterwheel, powered by the River Swilly, made five revolutions per minute and generated eight horsepower.

The entire operation could be handled by one miller, who knew every cog, lever, and flume in the joint. Call ahead to see when working mill demonstrations are scheduled; otherwise, tours last 20 minutes and are available on request.

Cost and Hours: Free, mid-May–mid-Sept daily 10:00-18:00, last entry 45 minutes before closing, closed off-season, Churchill Road, Letterkenny, tel. 074/912-5115.

• *Continue on R-250, staying right at Driminaught as the road becomes R-251. Watch for* Glenveagh Castle and National Park *signs, and park in the visitors center lot.*

▲▲Glenveagh Castle and National Park

One of Ireland's six national parks, Glenveagh's jewel is pristine Lough Veagh (Loch Ghleann Bheatha in Gaelic). The lake is three miles long, occupying a U-shaped valley scoured out of the Der-

ryveagh Mountains by powerful glaciers during the last Ice Age.

In the 1850s, this scenic area attracted the wealthy land speculator John George Adair, who bought the valley in 1857. Right away, Adair clashed with local tenants, whom he accused of stealing his sheep. After his managing agent was found murdered, he evicted all 244 of his bitter tenants to great controversy, and set about to create a hunting estate in grand Victorian style.

His pride and joy was his country mansion, Glenveagh Castle, finished in 1873 on the shore of Lough Veagh. After his death, his widow added to the castle and introduced rhododendrons and rare red deer to the estate. After her death, Harvard art professor Kingsley Porter bought the estate and promptly disappeared on the Donegal coast. (He's thought to have drowned.) The last owner was Philadelphia millionaire Henry McIlhenny, who filled the mansion with fine art and furniture while perfecting the lush surrounding gardens. He donated the castle to the Irish nation in 1981.

Cost and Hours: Park entry-free, guided castle tour-€5, daily mid-March-Oct 9:30-18:00, Nov-mid-March 9:00-17:00, last entry one hour before closing, tel. 0761/002-537, www.glenveagh-nationalpark.ie. Without a car, you can reach Glenveagh Castle and National Park by bus tour from Derry (see "Tours in Derry," earlier).

Visiting the Castle and National Park: The **Glenveagh National Park Visitors Centre** explains the region's natural history. Hiking trails in the park are scenic and tempting, but beware of the tiny midges that seem to want to nest in your nostrils.

The **castle** is only accessible by a 30-minute hike or a 10-minute shuttle-bus ride (€3 round-trip, 4/hour, depart from visitors center, last shuttle at 16:45). Take the 45-minute castle tour, letting your Jane Austen and Agatha Christie fantasies go wild. Antlers abound on walls, in chandeliers, and in paintings by Victorian hunting artists. A table crafted from rare bog oak (from ancient trees hundreds of years old, found buried in the muck) stands at attention in one room, while Venetian glass chandeliers illuminate a bathroom. A round pink bedroom at the top of a tower is decorated in Oriental style, with inlaid mother-of-pearl furnishings. The library, which displays paintings by George Russell, has the castle's best lake views.

Afterward, stroll through the gardens and enjoy the lovely setting. A lakeside swimming pool had boilers underneath it to keep it heated. It's no wonder that Greta Garbo was an occasional guest, coming to visit whenever she "vanted" to be alone.

• *Leave the national park and follow R-251 west, watching for the Mount Errigal trailhead. It's southeast of the mountain, and starts at the small parking lot beside R-251 on the mountain's lower slope (easy to spot, with a low surrounding stone wall in the middle of open bog land).*

Mount Errigal (An Earagail)

The mountain (2,400 feet) dominates the horizon for miles around. Rising from the relatively flat interior bog land, it looks taller from

a distance than it is. Beautifully cone-shaped (but not a volcano), it offers a hearty, non-technical climb with panoramic views (four hours round-trip, covering five miles). Hikers should get a weather report before setting out (frequent mists squat on the summit).

Donegal or Bust

Part of western County Donegal is in the Gaeltacht, where locals speak the Irish (Gaelic) language. In the spring of 2005, a controversial law was passed that erased all English place names from local road signs in Gaeltacht areas. Signs now only have the Irish-language equivalent, an attempt to protect the region from the further (and inevitable) encroachment of the English language.

Here's a cheat sheet to help you decipher the signs as you drive the Donegal loop (parts of which are in the Gaeltacht). There's also a complete translation of all Irish place names in the recommended *Complete Road Atlas of Ireland* by Ordnance Survey (€10), in the Gazetteer section in the back.

Gaelic Name	Pronounced	English Name
Leitir Ceanainn	*LET-ir CAN-ning*	Letterkenny
Min an Labain	*MEEN on law-BAWN*	Churchill
Loch Ghleann	*LOCKH thown*	Lough (Lake)
Bheatha	*eh-VEH-heh*	Veagh
An Earagail	*on AIR-i-gul*	Mt. Errigal
Gaoth Dobhair	*GWEE door*	Gweedore
Crothshli	*CROTH-lee*	Crolly
Bun Beag	*bun bee-OWG*	Bunbeg
Dori Beaga	*DOR-uh bee-OWG-uh*	Derrybeg
Cnoc Fola	*NOK FAW-luh*	Bloody Foreland
Gort an Choirce	*gurt on HER-kuh*	Gortahork
Dun Fionnachaidh	*doon on-AH-keh*	Dunfanaghy
Corran Binne	*COR-on BIN-eh*	Horn Head

• *Continue on R-251 as it merges into N-56 headed west; at Gweedore, stay west on R-258. After six kilometers (4 miles), you'll reach R-257, where you'll turn right and pass through the hamlet of Bunbeg (Bun Beag).*

The eight kilometers (5 miles) of road heading north—as Bunbeg blends into Derrybeg (Dori Beaga) and a bit beyond—are some of the most densely populated sections of this loop tour. Modern holiday cottages pepper the landscape in what the Irish have come to call "Bungalow Bliss" (or "Bungalow Blight" to nature lovers). Next you'll come to the...

Bloody Foreland (Cnoc Fola)

Named for the shade of red that backlit heather turns at sunset, this scenic headland is laced with rock walls and forgotten cottage ruins. Pull off at one of the lofty roadside viewpoints and savor a picnic lunch and rugged coastal views.

• *Continue on R-257, meeting N-56 near Gortahork. Stay on N-56 to the Dunfanaghy Workhouse, about a kilometer south of Dunfanaghy town.*

Dunfanaghy Workhouse

Opened in 1845, this structure was part of an extensive workhouse compound (separating families by gender and age)—a dreaded last resort for the utterly destitute of coastal Donegal. There were once many identical compounds built across Ireland, a rigid Victorian solution to the spiraling problem of Ireland's rapidly multiplying poor. Authorities at the time thought that poverty stemmed from laziness and should be punished. So, to motivate those lodging at the workhouse to pull themselves up by their bootstraps, conditions were made hard. But the system was unable to cope with the starving, homeless multitudes who were victims of the famine.

The harsh workhouse experience is told through the true-life narrative of Wee Hannah Herrity, a wandering orphan and former resident of this workhouse. During the famine, more than 4,000 young orphan workhouse girls from across Ireland were shipped to Australia as indentured servants in an attempt to offset the mostly male former convict population there. But Hannah's fate was different. She survived the famine by taking meager refuge here, dying at age 90 in 1926. With the audioguide, you'll visit three upstairs rooms where stiff papier-mâché figures relate the powerful episodes in her life.

Cost and Hours: €4.50, includes audioguide; June-Sept daily 9:30-17:30, shorter hours off-season, call to confirm winter hours, good bookstore and coffee shop, tel. 074/913-6540, www.dunfanaghyworkhouse.ie.

• *Now continue into the town of...*

Dunfanaghy (Dun Fionnachaidh)

This planned town, founded by the English in the early 1600s for local markets and fairs, has a prim and proper appearance. In Dunfanaghy (dun-FAN-ah-hee), you can grab a pub lunch or some picnic fixings from the town market. Enjoy them from a scenic viewpoint on the nearby Horn Head loop drive (described later).

The modest town square, mostly a parking lot, marks the center of Dunfanaghy. The post office is at the southern end of the village (Mon-Fri 9:00-17:30, Sat 9:00-13:00, closed Sun). Groceries

Irish Fishermen Feel the Squeeze

The biggest fishing port in Ireland is Killybegs, about 30 kilometers (19 miles) west of Donegal town. But today, fishing is a sadly withering lifestyle. When Ireland joined the EU in 1973, Irish farmers and infrastructure benefited most from generous subsidies that helped transform the country a generation later into the "Celtic Tiger." But as the country reaped over €35 billion from the EU in its first 25 years of membership, the Irish fishing industry suffered. With the Mediterranean overfished, other EU nations set sail for rich Irish waters that were newly opened to them. Some estimate that 40 percent of the fish caught each year in Europe—valued at €175 billion—come from Irish territorial seas. Huge factory ships from Spain are far more efficient at hauling in a catch than the 1,500 remaining Irish boats (most of which are under 40 feet long). Irish fishermen lament that for every €1 accepted in EU subsidies, €5 have gone out in foreign nets. And the irony is that much of the fish sold in Irish grocery stores and restaurants is now imported from other EU nations...who caught the fish off the Irish coast. Today, the biggest Irish fishing port may be the airport.

are sold in the **Centra Market** (Sun-Thu 7:30-21:00, Fri-Sat 7:30-22:00) on the main road opposite the town square.

Sleeping in Dunfanaghy: **$$$ The Mill Restaurant and Accommodation** is a diamond in the Donegal rough. Susan Alcorn nurtures six wonderful rooms with classy decor, while her husband Derek is the chef in their fine restaurant downstairs (Sb-€60-70, Db-€100-105, Tb-€120, Wi-Fi, parking, tel. 074/913-6985, www.themillrestaurant.com, info@themillrestaurant.com).

$$$ Arnold's Hotel is a comfortable old-fashioned place that's been in the Arnold family since 1922. In the center of town, its 31 cozy rooms are well-kept by a helpful staff (Sb-€55-70, Db-€110-140, Tb-€140-190, Qb-€150-200, occasional online discounts, all non-smoking, Wi-Fi, parking, tel. 074/913-6208, enquiries@arnoldshotel.com, www.arnoldshotel.com).

$$ The Whins B&B has three inviting rooms with tasteful furnishings, which range from exotic African accents to a sturdy four-poster bed (Sb-€35-45, Db-€70, Tb-€90-105, Wi-Fi, parking, 10-minute walk north of town, tel. 074/913-6481, mobile

086/162-3948, www.thewhins.com, annemarie@thewhins.com, Anne Marie Moore).

Eating in Dunfanaghy: **The Mill Restaurant and Accommodation** is gourmet all the way, specializing in memorable lamb or lobster dinners. It's worth booking days ahead of time (€45, Tue-Sun 19:00-21:00, closed Mon, tel. 074/913-6985). **Muck & Muffin** is a simple sandwich café, great for quick, cheap lunches. It's above the pottery shop in the stone warehouse on the town square (Mon-Sat 9:30-17:00—or until 18:00 mid-June-mid-Sept, Sun 10:30-17:00, tel. 074/913-6780). **The Great Wall** is a hole-in-the-wall Chinese takeaway place (daily 16:30-23:00, tel. 074/910-0111, next door to Centra Market). A few doors down, **The Oyster Bar** does pub grub and live music on Friday and Saturday nights.

• *From Dunfanaghy, you can head back to Derry via Letterkenny, but first consider a detour to Horn Head.*

Horn Head Loop (Corran Binne)

If you have extra time, take an hour to embark on a lost-world plateau drive. This heaving headland with few trees has memorable

coastal views that have made it popular with hikers in recent years.

Consult your map and get off N-56, following the Horn Head signs all the way around the eastern lobe of the peninsula. There are fewer than eight kilometers (5 miles) of narrow, single-lane road out here, with very little traffic. But be alert and willing to pull over at wide spots to cooperate with other cars.

This stone-studded peninsula was once an island. Then, shortly after the last Ice Age ended, ocean currents deposited a sandy spit in the calm water behind the island. A hundred years ago, locals harvested its stabilizing dune grass, using it for roof thatching and sending it abroad to Flanders, where soldiers used it to create beds for horses during World War I. However, with the grass gone, the sandy spit was free to migrate again. It promptly silted up the harbor, created a true peninsula, and ruined Dunfanaghy as a port town.

A short spur road leads to the summit of the headland, where you can park your car and walk another 50 yards up to the abandoned WWII lookout shelter. The views from here are dramatic, looking west toward Tory Island and south to Mount Errigal. Some may choose to hike an additional 20 minutes across the heather, to the ruins of the distant signal tower (not a castle, but instead a lookout for a feared Napoleonic invasion), clearly visible near the cliffs. New hiking trails are being created on the peninsula. But from here, it's still easy to bushwhack your way through (in sturdy footwear) to the rewarding cliff views at the base of old signal tower. Navigate back to your car, using the lookout shelter on the summit as a landmark.

PRACTICALITIES

This section covers just the basics on traveling in Northern Ireland (for much more information, see *Rick Steves' Ireland*). You can find free advice on specific topics at www.ricksteves.com/tips.

While it shares an island with the Republic of Ireland, Northern Ireland is part of the United Kingdom—which makes its currency, phone codes, and other practicalities different from the Republic. Keep in mind that County Donegal, described in this book as a handy side-trip from Derry, is actually in the Republic of Ireland.

Money

For currency, Northern Ireland uses the pound (£): 1 pound (£1) = about $1.60. One pound is broken into 100 pence (p). To convert prices in pounds to dollars, add about 60 percent: £20 = about $32, £50 = about $80. (Check www.oanda.com for the latest exchange rates.) While the pound used here is called the «Ulster Pound,» it›s interchangeable with the British pound. Note that County Donegal, in the Republic of Ireland, uses euros (€1 = about $1.30).

The standard way for travelers to get local currency is to withdraw money from ATMs (which locals may call «cash points») using a debit card, ideally with a Visa or MasterCard logo. Before departing, call your bank or credit-card company: Confirm that your card will work overseas, ask about international transaction fees, and alert them that you'll be making withdrawals in Europe. Also ask for the PIN number for your credit card in case it'll help you use Europe's "chip-and-PIN" payment machines (see below); allow time for your bank to mail your PIN to you. To keep your valuables safe, wear a money belt.

Dealing with "Chip and PIN": Much of Europe—including Northern Ireland—is adopting a "chip-and-PIN" system for credit cards, and some merchants rely on it exclusively. European chip-and-PIN cards are embedded with an electronic chip, in addition to the magnetic stripe used on our American-style cards. This means that your credit (and debit) card might not work at payment machines, such as those at train and subway stations, toll roads, parking garages, luggage lockers, and self-serve gas pumps. Memorizing your credit card's PIN lets you use it at some chip-and-PIN machines—just enter your PIN when prompted. If a payment machine won't take your card, look for a machine that takes cash or see if there's a cashier nearby who can process your transaction. Often the easiest solution is to pay for your purchases with cash you've withdrawn from an ATM using your debit card (Europe's ATMs still accept magnetic-stripe cards).

Phoning

Smart travelers use the telephone to reserve or reconfirm rooms, reserve restaurants, get directions, research transportation connections, confirm tour times, phone home, and lots more.

To call Northern Ireland from the US or Canada: Dial 011-44 and then 28 (Northern Ireland's area code, minus its initial zero), followed by the local number. (The 011 is our international access code, and 44 is the UK's country code.)

To call Northern Ireland from a European country: Dial 00-44 followed by 28 and the local number. (The 00 is Europe's international access code.)

To call within Northern Ireland and the UK: Since all of Northern Ireland shares one area code (028), all calls within the country are local—so you can leave off the area code and simply dial the local number. If you're calling to or from elsewhere in the UK, you need to include the area code.

Calling between Northern Ireland and the Republic of Ireland: To make calls from Northern Ireland to the Republic, dial 00-353, then the area code without its initial 0, then the local number. To call from the Republic to Northern Ireland, dial 048, then the local number (without the 028 area code).

To call from Northern Ireland to another country: Dial 00 followed by the country code (for example, 1 for the US or Canada), then the area code and number. If you're calling European countries whose phone numbers begin with 0, you'll usually have to omit that 0 when you dial.

Tips on Phoning: A mobile phone—whether an American one that works in Northern Ireland, or a European one you buy when you arrive—is handy, but can be pricey. If traveling with a

From:	rick@ricksteves.com
Sent:	Today
To:	info@hotelcentral.com
Subject:	Reservation request for 19-22 July

Dear Hotel Central,

I would like to reserve a room for 2 people for 3 nights, arriving 19 July and departing 22 July. If possible, I would like a quiet room with a double bed and a bathroom inside the room.

Please let me know if you have a room available and the price.

Thank you!
Rick Steves

smartphone, switch off data-roaming until you have free Wi-Fi. With Wi-Fi, you can use your smartphone to make free or inexpensive domestic and international calls by taking advantage of a calling app such as Skype or FaceTime.

Pay phones are relatively easy to find in Northern Ireland, but they're expensive. You'll pay with a major credit card (which you insert into the phone—minimum charge for a credit-card call is £1.20) or coins (have a bunch handy; minimum fee is £0.60).

You can buy international phone cards, which work with a scratch-to-reveal PIN code at any phone, allowing you to call home to the US for about a dime a minute (and also work for domestic calls within Northern Ireland). However, since you'll pay a big surcharge to use these cards from pay phones, they're cost-effective only if used from a landline (such as one at your B&B) or a mobile phone. For much more on phoning, see www.ricksteves.com/phoning.

Making Hotel and B&B Reservations

To ensure the best value, I recommend reserving rooms in advance, particularly during peak season. Email the hotelier or B&B host with the following key pieces of information: number and type of rooms; number of nights; date of arrival; date of departure; and any special requests. (For a sample form, see above image.) Use the European style for writing dates: day/month/year. For example, for a two-night stay in July, you could request: "1 double room for 2 nights, arrive 16/07/14, depart 18/07/14." Hoteliers typically ask for your credit-card number as a deposit.

Know the terminology: An "en suite" room has a bathroom (toilet and shower/tub) actually inside the room; a room with a "private bathroom" can mean that the bathroom is all yours, but it's across the hall. A "standard" room could have two meanings. Big hotels sometimes call a basic en-suite room a "standard" room to differentiate it from a fancier "superior" or "deluxe" room. At small hotels and B&Bs, guests in a "standard" room have access to a bathroom that's shared with other rooms and down the hall.

Given the economic downturn, hoteliers may be willing to make a deal—try emailing several hotels to ask for their best price. In general, hotel prices can soften if you do any of the following: stay in a "standard" room, offer to pay cash, stay at least three nights, or travel off-season.

Eating

The traditional "Ulster Fry" breakfast includes juice, tea or coffee, cereal, eggs, bacon, sausage, toast, a grilled tomato, sautéed mushrooms, and black pudding. If it's too much for you, order only the items you want.

To dine affordably at classier restaurants, look for "early-bird specials" (offered about 17:30–19:00, last order by 19:00). At a sit-down place with table service, tip about 10 percent—unless the service charge is already listed on the bill.

Smart travelers use pubs (short for "public houses") to eat, drink, and make new friends. Pub grub is Northern Ireland's best eating value. For about $15–20, you'll get a basic hot lunch or dinner. The menu is hearty and traditional: stews, soups, fish-and-chips, meat, cabbage, potatoes, and—in coastal areas—fresh seafood. Order drinks and meals at the bar. Pay as you order, and don't tip.

Most pubs have lagers (cold, refreshing, American-style beer), ales (amber-colored, cellar-temperature beer), bitters (hop-flavored ale, perhaps the most typical British beer), and stouts (dark and somewhat bitter—the most famous is Guinness, of course).

Transportation

By Car: A car is a worthless headache in Belfast. But if venturing into the countryside, I enjoy the freedom of a rental car for reaching far-flung rural sights. It's cheaper to arrange most car rentals from the US. For route planning, consult www.viamichelin.com, and for tips on your car insurance options, see www.ricksteves.com/cdw (if you're also going to the Republic of Ireland, note that many credit-card companies do not offer collision coverage for rentals in the Republic). Bring your driver's license.

Remember that people throughout Ireland drive on the left side of the road (and the driver sits on the right side of the car). You'll quickly master the many roundabouts: Traffic moves clockwise, cars inside the roundabout have the right-of-way, and entering traffic yields (look to your right as you merge). Note that "camera cops" strictly enforce speed limits by automatically snapping photos of speeders' license plates, then mailing them a bill.

Local road etiquette is similar to that in the US. Ask your car-rental company about the rules of the road, or check the US State Department website (www.travel.state.gov, click on "International Travel," then specify your country of choice and click "Traffic Safety and Road Conditions").

By Train and Bus: You can check train and bus schedules at www.translink.co.uk, or call 028/9066-6630. To see if a railpass could save you money, check www.ricksteves.com/rail. Long-distance buses (called "coaches") are about a third slower than trains, but they're also much cheaper. Bus stations are normally at or near train stations.

Helpful Hints

Emergency Help: To summon the **police** or an **ambulance,** dial 999. For passport problems, call the **US Consulate** (in Belfast, tel. 028/9038-6100). The **Canadian Consulate** in Belfast (tel. 028/9127-2060) does not offer passport services; instead contact the Canadian High Commission in London (02/072-586-600). For other concerns, get advice from your hotel.

Theft or Loss: To replace a passport, you'll need to go in person to an embassy or consulate (see above). Cancel and replace your credit and debit cards by calling these 24-hour US numbers collect: Visa—tel. 303/967-1096, MasterCard—tel. 636/722-7111, American Express—tel. 336/393-1111. File a police report either on the spot or within a day or two; you'll need it to submit an insurance claim for lost or stolen railpasses or travel gear, and it can help with replacing your passport or credit and debit cards. Precautionary measures can minimize the effects of loss—back up your digital photos and other files frequently. For more information, see www.ricksteves.com/help.

Time: Northern Ireland uses the 24-hour clock. It's the same through 12:00 noon, then keep going: 13:00, 14:00, and so on. Ireland, like Great Britain, is five/eight hours ahead of the East/West Coasts of the US (and one hour earlier than most of continental Europe).

Holidays and Festivals: Northern Ireland celebrates many holidays, which can close sights and attract crowds (book hotel rooms ahead). For information on holidays and festivals, check Ireland's tourism website: www.discoverireland.com. For a simple list showing major—though not all—events, see www.ricksteves.com/festivals.

Numbers and Stumblers: What Americans call the second floor of a building is the first floor in Northern Ireland. Local people write dates as day/month/year, so Christmas is 25/12/14. For most measurements, Northern Ireland uses the metric system: A kilogram is 2.2 pounds, and a liter is about a quart. For driving distances, they use miles (though the Republic is transitioning to kilometers on road signs—the speed limits are now given in kilometers per hour).

Resources from Rick Steves

This Snapshot guide is excerpted from my latest edition of *Rick Steves' Ireland*, which is one of more than 30 titles in my series of guidebooks on European travel. I also produce a public television series, *Rick Steves' Europe*, and a public radio show, *Travel with Rick Steves*. My website, www.ricksteves.com, offers free travel information, a forum for travelers' comments, guidebook updates, my travel blog, an online travel store, and information on European railpasses and our tours of Europe. If you're bringing a mobile device on your trip, you can download free information from Rick Steves Audio Europe, featuring podcasts of my radio shows, free audio tours of major sights in Europe, and travel interviews about Ireland (via www.ricksteves.com/audioeurope, iTunes, Google Play, or the Rick Steves Audio Europe free smartphone app). You can follow me on Facebook and Twitter.

Additional Resources

Tourist Information: www.discoverireland.com
Passports and Red Tape: www.travel.state.gov
Travel Insurance Tips: www.ricksteves.com/insurance
Packing List: www.ricksteves.com/packlist
Cheap Flights: www.kayak.com
Airplane Carry-on Restrictions: www.tsa.gov/travelers
Updates for This Book: www.ricksteves.com/update

How Was Your Trip?

If you'd like to share your tips, concerns, and discoveries after using this book, please fill out the survey at www.ricksteves.com/feedback. Thanks in advance—it helps a lot.

PRACTICALITIES

INDEX

INDEX

INDEX

Rick's Free Travel App

Get your FREE **Rick Steves Audio Europe**™ app to enjoy...

- Dozens of self-guided tours of Europe's top museums, sights and historic walks

- Hundreds of tracks filled with cultural insights and sightseeing tips from Rick's radio interviews

- All organized into handy geographic playlists

- For iPhone, iPad, iPod Touch, Android

With Rick whispering in your ear, Europe gets even better.

Find out more at ricksteves.com

Join a Rick Steves tour

Enjoy Europe's warmest welcome... with the flexibility and friendship of a small group getting to know Rick's favorite places and people. It all starts with our free tour catalog and DVD.

Great guides, small groups, no grumps.

Free information and great gear to

▶ Explore Europe

Browse thousands of articles, video clips, photos and radio interviews, plus find a wealth of money-saving tips for planning your dream trip. You'll find up-to-date information on Europe's best destinations, packing smart, getting around, finding rooms, staying healthy, avoiding scams and more.

▶ Travel News

Subscribe to our free Travel News e-newsletter, and get monthly updates from Rick on what's happening in Europe!

▶ Travel Forums

Learn, ask, share—our online community of savvy travelers is a great resource for first-time travelers to Europe, as well as seasoned pros.

Rick Steves' Europe Through the Back Door, Inc.

NOW AVAILABLE:
eBOOKS, DVD & BLU-RAY

TRAVEL CULTURE
Europe 101
European Christmas
Postcards from Europe
Travel as a Political Act

eBOOKS
Nearly all Rick Steves guides are available as eBooks. Check with your favorite bookseller.

RICK STEVES' EUROPE DVDs
11 New Shows 2013–2014
Austria & the Alps
Eastern Europe
England & Wales
European Christmas
European Travel Skills & Specials
France
Germany, BeNeLux & More
Greece, Turkey & Portugal
Iran
Ireland & Scotland
Italy's Cities
Italy's Countryside
Scandinavia
Spain
Travel Extras

BLU-RAY
Celtic Charms
Eastern Europe Favorites
European Christmas
Italy Through the Back Door
Mediterranean Mosaic
Surprising Cities of Europe

PHRASE BOOKS & DICTIONARIES
French
French, Italian & German
German
Italian
Portuguese
Spanish

JOURNALS
Rick Steves' Pocket Travel Journal
Rick Steves' Travel Journal

PLANNING MAPS
Britain, Ireland & London
Europe
France & Paris
Germany, Austria & Switzerland
Ireland
Italy
Spain & Portugal

Rick Steves books and DVDs are available at bookstores and through online booksellers.

Rick Steves

www.ricksteves.com

EUROPE GUIDES

Best of Europe
Eastern Europe
Europe Through the Back Door
Mediterranean Cruise Ports
Northern European Cruise Ports

COUNTRY GUIDES

Croatia & Slovenia
England
France
Germany
Great Britain
Ireland
Italy
Portugal
Scandinavia
Spain
Switzerland

CITY & REGIONAL GUIDES

Amsterdam, Bruges & Brussels
Barcelona
Budapest
Florence & Tuscany
Greece: Athens & the Peloponnese
Istanbul
London
Paris
Prague & the Czech Republic
Provence & the French Riviera
Rome
Venice
Vienna, Salzburg & Tirol

SNAPSHOT GUIDES

Berlin
Bruges & Brussels
Copenhagen & the Best of
    Denmark
Dublin
Dubrovnik
Hill Towns of Central Italy
Italy's Cinque Terre
Krakow, Warsaw & Gdansk
Lisbon
Madrid & Toledo
Milan & the Italian Lakes District
Munich, Bavaria & Salzburg
Naples & the Amalfi Coast
Northern Ireland
Norway
Scotland
Sevilla, Granada & Southern Spain
Stockholm

POCKET GUIDES

Athens
Barcelona
Florence
London
Paris
Rome
Venice

Rick Steves guidebooks are published by Avalon Travel,
a member of the Perseus Books Group.

Avalon Travel
a member of the Perseus Books Group
1700 Fourth Street
Berkeley, CA 94710

Text © 2013 by Rick Steves.
Maps © 2013 by Europe Through the Back Door.
Printed in Canada by Friesens.
First printing January 2014.
Portions of this book originally appeared in *Rick Steves' Ireland 2014*.

ISBN 978-1-61238-691-1

For the latest on Rick's lectures, guidebooks, tours, public radio show, and public television series, contact Europe Through the Back Door, Box 2009, Edmonds, WA 98020, tel. 425/771-8303, www.ricksteves.com, rick@ricksteves.com.

Europe Through the Back Door

Managing Editor: Risa Laib
Editorial & Production Manager: Jennifer Madison Davis
Editors: Glenn Eriksen, Tom Griffin, Cameron Hewitt, Deb Jensen, Suzanne Kotz, Cathy Lu, John Pierce, Carrie Shepherd
Editorial Assistant: Jessica Shaw
Editorial Intern: Zosha Milliman
Maps & Graphics: David C. Hoerlein, Lauren Mills, Dawn Tessman Visser, Laura VanDeventer

Avalon Travel

Senior Editor and Series Manager: Madhu Prasher
Editor: Jamie Andrade
Associate Editor: Annette Kohl
Assistant Editor: Maggie Ryan
Copy Editor: Denise Silva
Proofreader: Janet Walden
Indexer: Stephen Callahan
Cover Design: Kimberly Glyder Design
Maps & Graphics: Kat Bennett, Mike Morgenfeld

Cover Photo: ruins of Dunluce Castle, County Antrim, Northern Ireland © Richard Semik/123rf.com
Title Page Photo: ruins of Dunluce Castle, County Antrim, Northern Ireland © Richard Semik/www.123rf.com
Additional Photography: Pat O'Connor, Rick Steves, David C. Hoerlein, Dominic Bonuccelli, Wikimedia Commons

ABOUT THE AUTHORS

RICK STEVES

Since 1973, Rick Steves has spent 100 days every year exploring Europe. Along with writing and researching a bestselling series of guidebooks, Rick produces a public television series *(Rick Steves' Europe)*, a public radio show *(Travel with Rick Steves)*, and an app and podcast *(Rick Steves Audio Europe)*; writes a nationally syndicated newspaper column; organizes guided tours that take over ten thousand travelers to Europe annually; and offers an information-packed website (www.ricksteves.com). With the help of his hardworking staff of 80 at Europe Through the Back Door—in Edmonds, Washington, just north of Seattle—Rick's mission is to make European travel fun, affordable, and culturally enlightening for Americans.

Connect with Rick:

facebook.com/RickSteves twitter: @RickSteves

PAT O'CONNOR

Pat O'Connor, an Irish-American, first journeyed to Ireland in 1981 and was hooked by the history and passion of the feisty Irish culture. Frequent return visits led to his partnership with Rick, his work as an Ireland tour guide for Rick Steves' Europe Through the Back Door, and co-authorship of this book. Pat, who loves all things Hibernian except the black pudding, thrives on the adventures that occur as he slogs the bogs and drives the Irish back lanes (more than 2,000 kilometers annually) in search of new discoveries.

Want More Ireland?
Maximize the experience with Rick Steves as your guide

Guidebooks
London and Britain guides make side-trips smooth and affordable

Planning Maps
Use the map that's in sync with your guidebook

Rick's DVDs
Preview your destinations with 4 shows on Ireland

Free! Rick's Audio Europe™ App
Hear Ireland travel tips from Rick's radio shows

Small-Group Tours
Take a lively Rick Steves tour through Ireland

For all the details, visit ricksteves.com